Creating Your Strategic Plan

A Workbook for Public and Nonprofit Organizations

Third Edition

John M. Bryson and Farnum K. Alston

JOSSEY-BASS
A Wiley Imprint
www.josseybass.com

Published by Jossey-Bass
A Wiley Imprint
989 Market Street, San Francisco, CA 94103-1741—www.josseybass.com

Certain pages of this book may be customized and reproduced. The reproducible pages are designated by the appearance of the following copyright notice at the foot of each page:

This notice must appear on all reproductions as printed.

Readers should be aware that Internet Web sites offered as citations and/or sources for further information may have changed or disappeared between the time this was written and when it is read.

Jossey-Bass books and products are available through most bookstores. To contact Jossey-Bass directly call our Customer Care Department within the U.S. at 800-956-7739, outside the U.S. at 317-572-3986, or fax 317-572-4002.

Jossey-Bass also publishes its books in a variety of electronic formats. Some content that appears in print may not be available in electronic books.

ISBN: 978-0-470-40535-2 (paper)
ISBN: 978-1-118-06725-3 (ebk)

Printed in the United States of America
THIRD EDITION

PB Printing   10 9 8 7 6 5 4 3 2 1

Contents

Preface to the Third Edition

STRATEGIC PLANNING IS a way of life for the majority of public and nonprofit organizations. We are pleased to have played a role in bringing about that change through our publications and through the more than 500 major strategic planning processes we have helped facilitate since the publication of the first edition of this workbook in 1996 as a companion to the revised edition of *Strategic Planning for Public and Nonprofit Organizations* (Bryson, 1995). This third edition of the workbook accompanies the fourth edition of *Strategic Planning for Public and Nonprofit Organizations* (Bryson, 2011). The workbook has a new name—*Creating Your Strategic Plan* (rather than *Creating and Implementing Your Strategic Plan*)—because it is joined for the first time by a second workbook—*Implementing and Sustaining Your Strategic Plan*—that provides far more detailed information and worksheets about how to approach the challenge of implementing a strategic plan (see Bryson, Anderson, & Alston, 2011).

The basic approach we outlined in the first edition has proven as useful today as when we first proposed it. However, the field has changed as the world of theory and practice has evolved. This third edition embodies much of what we have learned since publication of the last edition.

Why has strategic planning become standard practice for most public and non-profit organizations? There are a variety of reasons. First, many public organizations are now required by law to undertake strategic planning, and many nonprofit organizations are required to do so by their funders. Second, strategic planning is now seen as a mark of good professional practice, so organizations pursue it to enhance their legitimacy. And many organizations simply copy what everyone else is doing. But we believe the most important reason strategic planning is so widely used is that public and nonprofit leaders find that it can *help* them to think, act, and learn strategically—precisely what is required for these leaders to grasp the challenges their organizations face, figure out what to do about them, and follow through with effective implementation. In short, strategic planning at its best fosters strategic thinking, acting, and learning and is a crucial component of change management.

The challenges are all too familiar. Public and nonprofit organizations and communities are confronted with a bewildering array of difficult situations requiring an effective response, including the following:

Changing and significantly increased—or reduced—demands for their programs, services, and products

Greater difficulty—and often much more difficulty—in acquiring the resources they need to fulfill their missions

The need to collaborate with other organizations and often across sector boundaries, so that somehow, competing organizational logics must be at least accommodated if not reconciled

A demand for greater accountability and good governance

More active and vocal stakeholders, including employees, customers, clients, funders, and citizens

Heightened (sometimes staggering) uncertainty about the future—in terms of the economy, politics, social and demographic changes, the environment, public safety, and so on—along with the subsequent need to assess risks and prepare for at least some of the possible contingencies

Pressures to restructure, reengineer, reframe, repurpose, or otherwise change themselves; to constantly improve the efficiency, effectiveness, equity, and quality of their processes; and to collaborate or compete with others more effectively to better serve key external or internal customers

The related need to make best use of the expanding array of information, communication, and social networking technologies

The need to integrate plans of many different kinds—strategic, business, budget, information technology, human resource management, and financial plans and also short-term action plans

Leaders and managers of organizations and communities must think, act, and learn strategically, now and in the future, if they are to meet their legal, ethical, professional, organizational, community, and public service obligations successfully. Taking a strategic planning approach is a must if these organizations and communities are to compete, survive, and prosper—and if real public value is to be created and the common good is to be served.

This workbook addresses key issues in the design of an overall strategic planning process, from the initial stages through plan preparation, review, and subsequent implementation and evaluation. However, it only touches on the major elements of these processes. We therefore recommend that this workbook be used in tandem with the fourth edition of *Strategic Planning for Public and Nonprofit Organizations* (Bryson, 2011), which places this workbook's and the accompanying implementation workbook's guidance and worksheets in a broader context, provides information on other significant issues, reviews relevant details, and alerts users to important caveats.

Furthermore, this workbook is not a substitute for the internal or external professional strategic planning consultation and facilitation services often needed during a strategic planning effort. The process of strategic planning is both important enough and difficult enough that having support from someone who has "been there and done that"—and who has thought wisely and reflectively about the process—may make the difference between a successful, high-value effort and one that stalls or fails or that even though completed does not produce high-value results.

Audience

This workbook is intended mostly for leaders, managers, planners, employees, and other stakeholders of public and nonprofit organizations and communities. We have found, however, that many people in private sector organizations have used the previous editions of this workbook, too, either because their organizations have a direct business relationship with public or nonprofit organizations or because they find the approach generally applicable to organizational strategic planning. We have also discovered that a surprising number of people use this approach to do personal strategic planning, that is, for themselves as individuals. The audience for the third edition of this workbook therefore includes

People interested in exploring the applicability of strategic planning to their organizations, networks, collaborations, or communities—and perhaps themselves

Sponsors, champions, and funders of strategic planning processes

Strategic planning teams

Strategic planning consultants and process facilitators

Teachers and students of strategic planning

Where This Workbook Will Be Relevant

This workbook is designed to be of use to a variety of people and groups working on developing a strategic plan for

Public and nonprofit organizations as whole entities (rather than their parts)

Parts of public and nonprofit organizations (departments, divisions, offices, bureaus, units)

Personnel involved with programs, projects, business processes, and functions (such as personnel, finance, purchasing, and information management) that cross departmental lines within an organization

Collaborations involving programs, projects, business processes, and services that involve more than one organization in often more than one sector

Networks or groups of organizations focused on cross-cutting functions or issues

Communities

On occasion, single individuals

The worksheets generally assume that the focus of the strategic planning effort is an organization. Please tailor and modify them appropriately if your focus is different.

How This Workbook Facilitates Strategic Planning

The workbook makes strategic planning easier in several ways, including the following:

The strategic planning process is *demystified* and made understandable and accessible. Although we have taken the risk of simplifying a complex process, this approach has been tested in hundreds of strategic planning efforts.

Fears about the process are allayed through the presentation of a simple, flexible model; step-by-step guidance; and easily understood worksheets.

Process sponsors, champions, consultants, and facilitators are provided with many of the tools they will need to guide an organization or group through a strategic process of thinking, acting, and learning.

The complex process of strategic planning has been broken down into manageable steps, making the overall strategy change process easier to manage.

Use of the workbook can document progress and keep the process on track.

Communication among process participants is made easier by the workbook's structured approach. Tangible products emerge from completing the worksheets, including the products necessary to develop a strategic plan. These products can guide the discussion and the process and substantiate the need for important changes.

Overview of the Contents

This workbook is divided into two sections:

- Part One presents an overview of the strategic planning and implementation process and the benefits to be gained by using it. The chapter on the context and process of strategic change includes readiness assessment worksheets.
- Part Two covers each of the ten key steps of the process in more detail. Each step description includes sections on purpose and possible desired planning outcomes and offers worksheets to facilitate the process.

The workbook ends with supportive resources, a glossary, and a bibliography.

Acknowledgments

JOHN WOULD LIKE TO THANK the people with whom he has worked over the years on various strategic planning projects. He has learned a great deal from them and appreciates their willingness to help him understand more about strategic planning and how to make it more effective. He would also like to thank all the people who have taken his classes and workshops in strategic planning. And he is especially appreciative of Farnum Alston's contributions and willingness to bring his insights, experience, and talents to bear on this workbook project. He is a master strategic planning practitioner and theorist. Farnum has field-tested the contents of this workbook in an extraordinary number of settings. Finally, John would like to thank Barbara Crosby, for her special insights, constant encouragement, and love throughout the process of developing this third edition, and the other members of his delightfully expanding family, which now includes a grandchild. They provide more than enough inspiration to work for a better future for us all.

FARNUM WOULD FIRST LIKE TO THANK his family—his wife, Kirsten, and his daughter, Greer, for their love and support and their giving up of family time to allow him to continue to collaborate with John on this third edition of this workbook. He would next like to thank the many colleagues, clients, and friends who, over thirty-five years and now over 400 major organizational change management and strategic planning projects, have been the real-life inspiration for his work and his contribution to this workbook. Their hands-on involvement in public, private, and nonprofit organizations and their belief in better governance, quality leadership, integrity, honesty, and the need to add real value have been invaluable to him and to his contribution to this book. The colleagues include (among many) Steve Born, Bud Jordahl, Dale Stanway, William Bechtel, and Dave Schwartz. Special thanks go again to John Bryson. After thirty-five years of friendship we have come together for the third time to write this workbook. John's contributions to and insights about improving public and private organizations and their leadership and good governance have helped us all. On a final note, Farnum would like to extend special additional recognition to Bud (Harold) Jordahl Jr., an emeritus professor at the University of Wisconsin. Bud, who passed away at age eighty-three in May 2010, was a public policy legend in the environmental movement. He was also a key architect and a gentle guide in the careers of many, including Farnum's own. He is missed.

April 2011

John M. Bryson
Minneapolis, Minnesota

Farnum K. Alston
Bozeman, Montana

The Authors

John M. Bryson is McKnight Presidential Professor of Planning and Public Affairs in the Hubert H. Humphrey School of Public Affairs at the University of Minnesota. He works in the areas of leadership, strategic management, and the design of organizational and community change processes. He has consulted with a wide range of government, nonprofit, and business organizations in North America and Europe. He wrote the best-selling and award-winning *Strategic Planning for Public and Nonprofit Organizations*, now in its fourth edition (2011), and cowrote, with Barbara C. Crosby, the award-winning *Leadership for the Common Good*, second edition (2005). He is a Fellow of the National Academy of Public Administration.

Bryson has received many awards for his work, including four best book awards, three best article awards, the General Electric Award for Outstanding Research in Strategic Planning from the Academy of Management, and the Distinguished Research Award and the Charles H. Levine Memorial Award for Excellence in Public Administration given jointly by the National Association of Schools of Public Affairs and Administration and the American Society for Public Administration (ASPA). In 2011 he received the Dwight Waldo Award from ASPA. The award honors persons who have made "outstanding contributions to the professional literature of public administration over an extended scholarly career of at least 25 years." He serves on the editorial boards of the *American Review of Public Administration*, *International Public Management Journal*, *Public Management Review*, *International Review of Public Administration*, and *Journal of Public Affairs Education*.

He earned his undergraduate degree, in economics, from Cornell University, and he holds MS and PhD degrees in urban and regional planning and an MA degree in public policy and administration, all from the University of Wisconsin.

Farnum K. Alston is the founder of The Crescent Company—750 Black Bear Road, Bozeman, Montana 59718; phone (406) 600-6622; e-mail: f.alston@comcast .net. He established this company in 2000 to assist public, for-profit, and nonprofit organizations and also individuals with change management and strategic planning projects. Alston has, over the last forty years, worked on over 400 major change management and strategic planning projects for public, private, and nonprofit organizations. He has been a managing director for The International Center for Economic Growth and has served on many boards and committees of public and nonprofit organizations, including the Government Finance Officers Association (GFOA) award committee, the Baldrige National Awards evaluation committee, the Henry's Fork Foundation board (an environmental protection organization), the Going To The Sun Rally board (a nonprofit that raises money for good causes), and as an appointed member of several school district boards. He is also a recipient of the U.S. Department of Commerce Outstanding Service Award.

Alston has had extensive government experience at the federal, state, regional, and local levels. He served as (in chronological order) environmental adviser to Governor Patrick Lucey of Wisconsin, staff director of the federal Upper Great Lakes Regional Commission, director of the Upper Great Lakes Regional Commission (appointed by Presidents Ford and Carter), deputy chief administrative officer for the City and County of San Francisco, and deputy mayor and budget director for Dianne Feinstein when she was mayor of San Francisco.

Alston has also had extensive business experience, including being involved with over 200 major government and business consulting projects while working with Woodward Clyde Consultants; being a partner at KPMG Peat Marwick, where he led that organization's government and higher education sector practices; and being the founder and owner of The Resources Company and The Crescent Company.

Alston did his undergraduate work at the University of California, Berkeley, in economics and his postgraduate work at Montana State University and then at the University of Wisconsin, Madison, in public policy.

Part 1

An Overview

Introduction

What Is Strategic Planning and Why Do It?

Strategic planning is "a deliberative, disciplined effort to produce fundamental decisions and actions that shape and guide what an organization (or other entity) is, what it does, and why it does it" (Bryson, 2011). Strategic planning is an approach to dealing with the serious challenges that organizations, parts of organizations, collaborations, and communities face. These challenges require deliberation and discipline on the part of leaders if they are to be effectively managed.

All organizations are in a constant state of change and flux—even those that think of themselves as stable are typically changing in various ways. People are coming and going, mandates are shifting, budgets are changing, stakeholder needs and expectations are changing, and so on. A strategically managed organization is one that both defines where it wants to be and manages change effectively through an action agenda to achieve that future.

- Strategic planning is a way of thinking, acting, and learning.

- It usually takes a comprehensive view by focusing on the *big picture*, but it also leads to specific, targeted actions in the present in light of their longer-term consequences.

- It is often visionary and usually proactive rather than reactive in addressing the need for change.

- It is flexible and practical.

- It is a guide for decision making and resource allocation; strategic planning guides budgeting, not the reverse.

Strategic planning is not any one *thing* but is instead a *set* of concepts, procedures, methodologies, and tools that can help public and nonprofit organizations, collaborations, and communities to become more successful in defining and achieving their mission or vision and in creating significant and enduring public value.

Through strategic planning organizations can

- Document and discuss the environment in which they exist and operate, and explore the factors and trends that affect the way they do business and carry out their roles.

- Clarify and frame the issues or challenges facing the organization.

- Clarify organizational mission, goals, and values, and articulate a vision for where the organization wants to be.

- Develop strategies to meet their mandates, fulfill their missions, achieve their goals, be true to their values, realize their visions, and create public value by reexamining and reworking organizational mandates, mission, values, goals, product or service level and mix, clients, users or payers, cost, financing, structure, processes, or management.

To be effective, strategic planning must be action and results oriented and must be linked to operational planning. It must also be linked to a variety of *functional* types of planning—information technology, human resource, financing, business plans, and so forth. And planning of all types must be done with implementation in mind and the implementation process itself must be effectively managed; otherwise, hopes and dreams will amount to little more than idle fantasy.

Several Complementary Ways of Looking at and Thinking About Strategic Planning

Strategic planning is a process that typically results in a plan—and the process itself needs to be thought about strategically and often planned as well. Indeed, the process can be as important as any resulting plan. We have developed several complementary ways of viewing strategic planning, in order to both describe the process and help people understand what is involved. Different views will resonate with different people. These views are

The ABCs of strategic planning

The building-block view

The strategic planning process cycle

The project management view

The Strategy Change Cycle (presented in the next chapter)

The creating public value view (presented in the next chapter)

The ABCs of Strategic Planning

Throughout its strategic planning process, an organization must ask itself three fundamental questions (Figure 1):

FIGURE 1

The ABCs of Strategic Planning

Source: *Adapted from material developed by Farnum Alston and The Crescent Company, Bozeman, Montana.*

A. Who and what are we, what do we do now, and why?

The answers to this first question document the organization's current condition and establish the baseline from which to develop the strategic plan. Planning process participants often think they already know all this information, but when the question is explored and the answers are documented in a systematic way, participants almost invariably find they didn't know it all, much is learned, and many new insights emerge. Just as preliminary thinking about form and function affects the quality of the foundation of a building, the better the job you do in exploring this question at the start of your planning effort, the better the foundation for the overall plan and subsequent changes will be.

B. What do we want to be and do in the future, and why?

This second question puts a stake in the ground. It asks, where do we and other stakeholders want to be in the future, given where we are now? Yogi Berra said, "You've got to be very careful if you don't know where you're going, because you might not get there." A strategically managed organization takes a different tack when its members identify a desired direction and proactively work together to get there via effective strategies and implementation processes.

C. How do we get from here to there?

The answers to this question tell us how we close the gap between where we are and where we want to be. The gap consists of the strategic issues the organization needs to address. These issues must first be identified and then addressed by formulating and implementing strategies and actions that respond effectively to the issues.

•   •   •

Asking and answering these questions requires an ongoing, iterative, deliberative conversation among strategic planning team members and other key stakeholders. As the conversation unfolds, new answers to one question can be expected to change previous answers to other questions. The ten-step process and the worksheets presented in this workbook provide a reasonable and structured approach to answering these questions.

The conversation should be guided by keeping in mind the requirements for effective implementation—*not* by jumping to premature conclusions about what the best strategies to implement might be. Strategies should be seen as responses to challenges—the issues—and these challenges must be clearly understood before developing any strategies to address them. Typically, effective dialogue among knowledgeable people is required to clarify what the issues are and what the desirable, implementable strategies for addressing them might be.

The Building-Block View

Although a strategic planning process can start at several places, we have found that a visual model is helpful in presenting the elements—or *building blocks*—of a strategic planning process and plan and the phases that most processes go through (Figure 2).

Although the building blocks generally fit together logically within the phases, several different building blocks from different phases may be worked on at any one time. Regardless of the way this work is arranged, effective implementation has to rest on a strong foundation—and the foundation should be laid with implementation in mind.

FIGURE 2

The Building-Block View of Strategic Planning

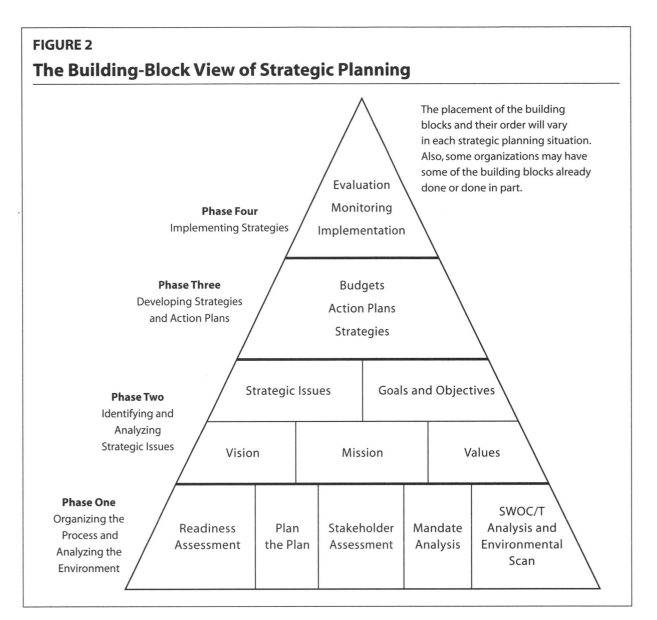

Phase Four
Implementing Strategies

Evaluation
Monitoring
Implementation

The placement of the building blocks and their order will vary in each strategic planning situation. Also, some organizations may have some of the building blocks already done or done in part.

Phase Three
Developing Strategies and Action Plans

Budgets
Action Plans
Strategies

Phase Two
Identifying and Analyzing Strategic Issues

Strategic Issues | Goals and Objectives

Vision | Mission | Values

Phase One
Organizing the Process and Analyzing the Environment

Readiness Assessment | Plan the Plan | Stakeholder Assessment | Mandate Analysis | SWOC/T Analysis and Environmental Scan

Source: *Adapted from material developed by Farnum Alston and The Crescent Company, Bozeman, Montana.*

The four phases are

1. Organizing the planning process and analyzing the environment

2. Identifying and analyzing strategic issues

3. Developing strategies and action plans that fulfill the mission, meet the mandates, and achieve desirable goals and objectives

4. Implementing strategies

Each of these four general phases consists of several building blocks of project activity and information that will result in a specific planning product.

Although some organizations may have some of these building blocks in place already, we have found that revisiting and documenting them within a structured strategic planning process is extremely helpful—particularly when the process involves new participants. For example, many organizations are convinced they already know what their mission and mandates are now and should be in the future. Our experience, however, is quite different. Typically, a large fraction of the organization's stakeholders display considerable ambiguity about or even ignorance of the mission and mandates.

In phase 1 the foundation is laid for the overall strategic plan itself.

- Readiness assessment

In conducting a readiness assessment, the organization explores its capacity to do strategic planning and implement the results. We have assisted many organizations who got into a planning process without conducting an appropriate readiness assessment and ended up trying to use a hammer when they needed a saw. It is important to be candid and ask the tough organizational questions before embarking on a strategic planning project.

- Plan the plan

The time spent on planning the plan is almost always well spent. As with building a home, you need to think through the process. Take the time to do this part of the process carefully, and it will pay off many times over the course of the project.

- Stakeholder assessment

- Mandate analysis

- Assessment of internal strengths and weaknesses and external opportunities and challenges (or threats)

Phase 2 establishes a clear sense of direction for the organization, as planners look at

- Vision, mission, and values

- Strategic issues, goals, and objectives

Phase 3 shows in more detail how the organization will address the issues it faces and build effective bridges from itself to its environment via

- Strategies

- Action plans

- Budgets

Phase 4 is where the ultimate payoffs are achieved and assessed, through

- Implementation

- Monitoring

- Evaluation

The Strategic Planning Process Cycle

The building-block view of strategic planning will seem too static for some. The cyclical nature of strategic planning is shown in Figure 3. The cycle is organized around an evolving sense of who the stakeholders are and what they want and of the mission, mandates, vision, and goals that emerge. It involves

- Planning the process
- Establishing mission and mandates and assessing the internal and external environments
- Identifying strategic issues
- Formulating strategies and an action agenda
- Reviewing and adopting a strategic plan
- Implementing and reassessing the plan
- Beginning the cycle anew

The Project Management View

Strategic planning may also be thought of in operational terms, because it is often conceived and organized as a *project*. Exhibit 1 presents a list of tasks and timelines for implementing an action that strategic planning has identified.

Two other views of strategic planning are presented in the next chapter. The Strategy Change Cycle is the ten-step process used to organize this workbook. The creating public value view shows how those ten steps can contribute to creating public value.

The Benefits of Strategic Planning

Strategic planning is intended to enhance an organization's ability to think, act, and learn strategically. The potential benefits from the process are numerous, although there is no guarantee that they will be realized in practice. These benefits include

- *Increased effectiveness.* The organization's performance is enhanced, its mission is furthered, its mandates are met, its values are honored, and real public value is created. In addition, the organization responds effectively to rapidly changing circumstances.
- *Increased efficiency.* The same or better results are achieved with fewer resources.
- *Improved understanding and better learning.* The organization understands its situation far more clearly. It is able to reconceptualize its situation and work, if necessary, and to establish an interpretive framework that can guide strategy development and implementation.
- *Better decision making.* A coherent, focused, and defensible basis for decision making is established, and today's decisions are made in light of their future consequences.

FIGURE 3

The Strategic Planning Process Cycle

The strategic planning process is typically cyclical and can begin at many places.

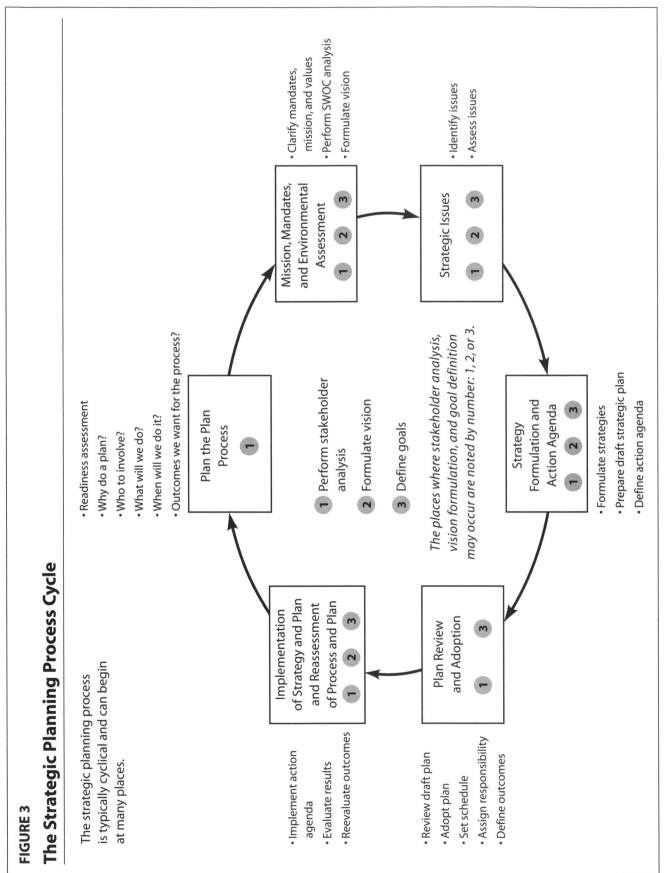

Plan the Plan Process ①

- Readiness assessment
- Why do a plan?
- Who to involve?
- What will we do?
- When will we do it?
- Outcomes we want for the process?

Mission, Mandates, and Environmental Assessment ① ② ③

- Clarify mandates, mission, and values
- Perform SWOC analysis
- Formulate vision

Strategic Issues ① ② ③

- Identify issues
- Assess issues

① Perform stakeholder analysis

② Formulate vision

③ Define goals

The places where stakeholder analysis, vision formulation, and goal definition may occur are noted by number: 1, 2, or 3.

Strategy Formulation and Action Agenda ① ② ③

- Formulate strategies
- Prepare draft strategic plan
- Define action agenda

Plan Review and Adoption ① ③

- Review draft plan
- Adopt plan
- Set schedule
- Assign responsibility
- Define outcomes

Implementation of Strategy and Plan and Reassessment of Process and Plan ① ② ③

- Implement action agenda
- Evaluate results
- Reevaluate outcomes

Source: *Adapted from material developed by Farnum Alston and The Crescent Company, Bozeman, Montana.*

EXHIBIT 1

The Project Management View of Strategic Planning: Implementation and Action Plan Example

Action	Key Steps or Tasks	Due Dates	Responsible Party and Involved Parties	Resources and Outcomes		
				People	Funding	Measurable Outcomes
Example:						
1. Educate department managers and staff on the roles and responsibilities of the ABC organizational strategy.	1. Update educational materials	Jan. 24	Organization training manager, ABC trainer, department trainers	.5 PY time	Printing costs	Document produced
	2. Determine date for 1 day of training	Feb. 24	ABC program trainer, department reps	Book facilitation help, room, and 20 people for the day	Meeting room and materials	Date established and facilities and facilitator booked
	3. Design the 1-day training event	Feb. 10	ABC trainer	3 days effort	NA	Meeting design
	4. Hold training event	Feb. 24	ABC trainer and department helpers	1 day meeting	NA	Training held and evaluations are positive
	5. Follow-up	Mar. 2	ABC trainer and organization management	2 hours ABC trainer and senior managers	NA	Good meeting and process assessment; action plans for having another training session if needed

Source: *Adapted from project management work plans developed by Farnum Alston and The Crescent Company, Bozeman, Montana.*

- *Enhanced organizational capabilities.* Broadly based organizational leadership is improved, and the capacity for further strategic thought, action, and learning is enhanced.

- *Improved communications and public relations.* Mission, vision, values, goals, strategies, and action programs are communicated more effectively to key stakeholders. A desirable image for the organization is established and managed.

- *Increased political support.* The organization's legitimacy is enhanced, its advocacy base broadened, and a powerful and supportive coalition developed.

Poor Excuses for Avoiding Strategic Planning

A number of reasons can be offered for not engaging in strategic planning. Too often, however, these "reasons" are actually excuses for avoiding necessary action. For example:

- *We don't have policy board support.* Think strategically about how to gain this board's support, perhaps for an effort aimed at addressing a single issue.

- *There's no top management support.* Again, think strategically about how to win management support.

- *Strategic planning won't fix everything or lead to perfection.* Of course it won't, and in fact it should not address everything! Taking on too many challenges at once can overwhelm the process and the organization's capacity to manage change, but most organizations can identify and address a limited number (five to ten) of high-priority challenges.

- *We're too big (or too small) for strategic planning.* If the U.S. Navy, the Internal Revenue Service, and the smallest nonprofits can benefit from strategic planning—which they do—size is not a legitimate argument for avoiding it.

- *We've got a union.* Then treat the union as another stakeholder.

- *We have personnel policies and individual performance goals to take care of this.* Think strategically about personnel policies, and ask whether or not the individual performance goals support desirable organizational strategies.

- *We don't know where to start.* You can start anywhere. The process is so interconnected that you will find yourselves covering most phases through conversation and dialogue, no matter where you start.

- *We've already done it*—some years ago. Times change. Revisit what you've done to see if it is still relevant.

- *We're perfect already!* Then you *really* need to be careful, because nothing breeds failure like success and the complacency that often comes with it.

Two Legitimate Reasons Not to Undertake Strategic Planning

Strategic planning is not always advisable for an organization. There are two compelling reasons for holding off on a strategic planning effort:

1. Strategic planning may not be the best first step for an organization whose roof has fallen. For example, the organization may need to remedy a cash flow crunch or fill a key leadership position before undertaking strategic planning.

2. If the organization lacks the skills or the resources or the commitment of key decision makers to carry through an effective strategic planning process and produce a good plan, the effort should not be undertaken. If strategic planning is attempted in such a situation, it should probably be a focused and limited effort aimed at developing those skills, resources, and commitments.

For strategic planning to succeed you need to be clear about whether strategic planning is what is needed, and if so, what kind of strategic planning process will help. You need to do a thorough readiness assessment first, such as the one discussed in the next chapter. That will help you figure out whether strategic planning is needed for the whole organization, part of the organization, an organizational function or issue, a collaboration, a community, or some other focus. It will also help you clarify what you might need to do *before* engaging in more formal strategic planning, such as acquire the support of key leaders, find necessary resources, do some training, or broaden the base of support beyond key leaders.

The Context and Process of Strategic Change

The Strategy Change Cycle: An Effective Strategic Planning Approach for Public and Nonprofit Organizations

This workbook is organized around a strategic planning and implementation process, the Strategy Change Cycle, that has proved effective for many public and nonprofit organizations. The Strategy Change Cycle is designed to help organizations meet their mandates, fulfill their missions, and create public value. The ten steps of the cycle are presented in Figure 4. The steps are as follows.

STEP 1: Initiate and Agree on a Strategic Planning Process

The purpose of Step 1 is to negotiate agreement with key internal (and possibly external) decision makers or opinion leaders on the overall strategic planning process, the desired outcomes, the schedule, the key planning tasks, and the likely requirements for success.

Some person or group must initiate the process. One of this person's or group's first important tasks is to identify the key decision makers, including the person or group likely to be the strategic planning process sponsor (SPS) and the person likely to be the strategic planning process champion (SPC). The next task is to determine which persons, groups, units, or organizations should be involved in the effort. The initial agreement will be negotiated with at least some of these decision makers, groups, units, or organizations.

FIGURE 4

The Strategy Change Cycle

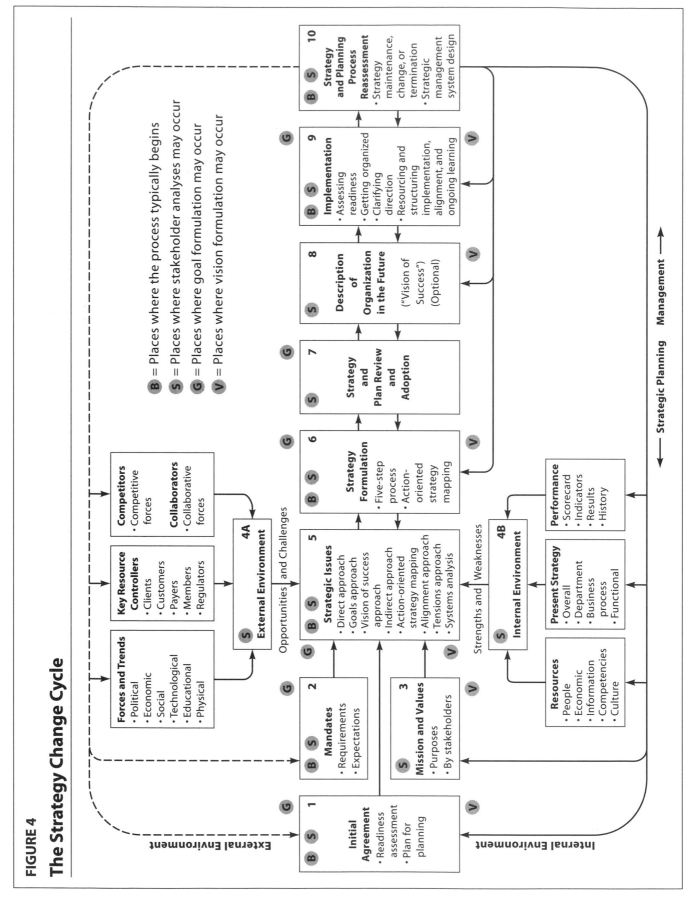

B = Places where the process typically begins
S = Places where stakeholder analyses may occur
G = Places where goal formulation may occur
V = Places where vision formulation may occur

Forces and Trends
- Political
- Economic
- Social
- Technological
- Educational
- Physical

Key Resource Controllers
- Clients
- Customers
- Payers
- Members
- Regulators

Competitors
- Competitive forces

Collaborators
- Collaborative forces

S **4A External Environment**

Opportunities and Challenges

External Environment

B S **2 Mandates**
- Requirements
- Expectations

S **3 Mission and Values**
- Purposes
- By stakeholders

B S **1 Initial Agreement**
- Readiness assessment
- Plan for planning

B G S **5 Strategic Issues**
- Direct approach
- Goals approach
- Vision of success approach
- Indirect approach
- Action-oriented strategy mapping
- Alignment approach
- Tensions approach
- Systems analysis

B S **6 Strategy Formulation**
- Five-step process
- Action-oriented strategy mapping

S **7 Strategy and Plan Review and Adoption**

S **8 Description of Organization in the Future** ("Vision of Success") (Optional)

B S **9 Implementation**
- Assessing readiness
- Getting organized
- Clarifying direction
- Resourcing and structuring implementation, alignment, and ongoing learning

B S **10 Strategy and Planning Process Reassessment**
- Strategy maintenance, change, or termination
- Strategic management system design

Strengths and Weaknesses

S **4B Internal Environment**

Internal Environment

Present Strategy
- Overall
- Department
- Business process
- Functional

Performance
- Scorecard
- Indicators
- Results
- History

Resources
- People
- Economic
- Information
- Competencies
- Culture

← Strategic Planning   Management →

16

Before a strategic planning effort is begun, however, it may be useful to perform a readiness assessment. The purpose of such an assessment is to determine how capable the organization is of undertaking a strategic planning effort and whether additional capacity may be needed. See Worksheets 1 through 7 at the end of this chapter and Resource A.

The strategic planning process agreement itself should cover

- The purpose of the effort
- A statement (however sketchy) of desired outcomes to be achieved
- The preferred steps in the process
- The schedule
- The form and timing of reports
- The role, functions, and membership of any group or committee empowered to oversee the effort (strategic planning coordinating committee, or SPCC)
- The role, functions, and membership of the strategic planning team (SPT)
- The likely requirements for success
- Any important limitations on or boundaries for the effort
- The commitment of resources necessary to proceed with the effort

See Worksheets 8 through 15.

STEP 2: Clarify Organizational Mandates

The purpose of this step is to clarify the formal and informal mandates placed on the organization (the *musts* and *must nots* it confronts) and to explore their implications for organizational action.

See Worksheets 16 and 17.

STEP 3: Identify and Understand Stakeholders, Develop and Refine Mission and Values, and Consider Developing a Vision Sketch

A stakeholder is any person, group, or entity that can place a claim on the organization's attention, resources, or output or that is affected by that output. The key to success for public and nonprofit organizations is the ability to address the needs and desires of crucial stakeholders—according to those stakeholders' criteria.

The organization's mission, in tandem with its mandates, provides its raison d'être and its principal route to creating public value. Any government, corporation, agency, or nonprofit organization must seek to meet certain identifiable social or political needs. Viewed in this light, an organization must always be considered the means to an end, not an end in and of itself.

The mission statement developed and refined in this step should grow out of a thorough consideration of who the organization's (or community's) stakeholders are. The organization's value system might also be identified, discussed, and documented. The organization may also wish to create a sketch of its *vision of success*, to guide subsequent planning efforts.

See Worksheets 18 through 26.

STEP 4: Assess the Environment to Identify Strengths, Weaknesses, Opportunities, and Challenges

In this step the strengths and weaknesses of the organization are catalogued and evaluated and their strategic implications noted. This may include identifying the organization's distinctive competencies—that is, those abilities that enable it to perform well against key performance indicators (or critical success factors), especially when compared to its competitors. In addition, the opportunities and challenges (or threats) facing the organization are explored, and again, strategic implications are recognized.

See Worksheets 27 through 31 and Resources F, G, and H.

STEP 5: Identify and Frame Strategic Issues

Together, the first four steps of the process lead to the fifth, the identification of strategic issues—the fundamental challenges affecting the organization's mandates, its mission and values, its product or service level and mix, its costs, its financing, its structure, its processes, and its management.

See Worksheets 32 through 35 and Resources F, G, and H.

STEP 6: Formulate Strategies to Manage the Issues

Strategies are developed to deal with the issues identified in Step 5. Strategies may be of several types:

- Grand (or umbrella) strategy for the organization, collaboration, network, or community as a whole

- Strategy for organizational subunits

- Strategies for one or more programs, services, products, projects, or business processes

- Strategies for one or more functions, such as human resource management, information technology, finance, or purchasing

These strategies can be used to set the context for other change efforts aimed at restructuring, reengineering, reframing, repurposing, or otherwise changing the organization.

See Worksheets 36 through 39.

Steps 1 through 6 may be thought of as strategic *planning*, whereas Steps 7 through 10 are more about *management*. All the steps together may be thought of as a *strategic management process*.

STEP 7: Review and Adopt the Strategic Plan

The purpose of this step is to gain a formal commitment to adopt and proceed with implementation of the plan(s). This step represents the culmination of the work of the previous steps and points toward the implementation step, in which adopted strategies are realized in practice. Formal adoption may not be necessary in all cases to gain the benefits of strategic planning, but quite often it is.

See Worksheets 40 and 41.

STEP 8: Establish an Effective Organizational Vision for the Future

An organization's vision of success outlines what the organization should look like as it successfully implements its strategies and achieves its full potential. Such a description, to the extent that it is widely known and agreed on in the organization, allows organizational members to know what is expected of them without constant direct managerial oversight. This description also allows other key stakeholders to know what the organization envisions for itself. Visions of success may be developed at several places in the process—and worksheets in previous steps should have prompted planning process participants to think about aspects of their vision for the future—but Step 8 is often where that thinking happens. Most organizations will not be able to develop an effective vision of success until they have gone through strategic planning more than once. Thus their vision of success is more likely to serve as a guide for strategy implementation than as a guide for strategy formulation.

See Worksheet 42.

STEP 9: Develop an Effective Implementation Process

In this step, adopted strategies are implemented throughout the relevant systems. An effective implementation process and action plan must be developed if the strategic plan is to be something other than an organizational New Year's resolution. The more that strategies have been formulated with implementation in mind and the more active the involvement of those required to implement the plan, the more successful strategy implementation is likely to be.

See Worksheets 43 through 49. Note as well that the companion workbook, *Implementing and Sustaining Your Strategic Plan* (Bryson, Anderson, & Alston, 2011), includes additional guidance and worksheets for pursuing Steps 9 and 10 of the strategy change process.

STEP 10: Reassess Strategies and the Strategic Planning Process

The purpose of this final step is to review implemented strategies and the strategic planning process. The aim is to find out what worked, what did not work, and why, and to set the stage for the next round of strategic planning.

See Worksheets 50 and 51.

The Strategy Change Cycle: Theory Versus Practice

Although the process is laid out here in a linear, sequential manner, it must be emphasized that in practice the process is typically iterative: participants usually rethink what they have done several times before they reach final decisions. Moreover, the process does not always begin at the beginning. Organizations may find themselves confronted with a serious strategic issue or a failing strategy that leads them to engage in strategic planning, and only later do they do Step 1.

It is also important to note that strategic planning efforts necessarily take place within a given context, even if the purpose of the effort is to change the context. Unless strategic planning is being used to design a brand-new organization, it will occur within ongoing processes of organizational change (which are typically cyclical or nonlinear) and must fit those processes. These include budgeting cycles, legislative cycles, the governing board's decision-making routines, and other change initiatives: for example, process improvement initiatives, information technology upgrades, or personnel system reforms.

There are also different levels of organizational change, ranging from the more abstract or conceptual (such as changes in mission, vision, and general goals) to the more specific or concrete (such as changes in work plans and budgets). Change may be orchestrated from the top, proceeding *deductively* down to the more concrete and specific level, or change may be initiated at the more concrete level, rising *inductively* toward the more abstract or conceptual level. Most often, change involves a combination of deductive and inductive approaches, and these must be blended as wisely as possible (Mintzberg, Ahlstrand, & Lampel, 2009; Mintzberg & Westley, 1992). For example, strategy formulation typically involves thinking about the practicalities of implementation prior to deciding on the strategies it will be wisest to pursue.

It is extremely important to note that, as indicated in Figure 4, goal formulation and visioning activities may be inserted at many points in the process, depending on the circumstances. As often as not, goal formulation comes later in the process, when strategies are formulated. Goals developed at that point will reflect the thrusts of specific strategies. Goals agreed on earlier in the process may well be too vague to serve as useful guides for action. Nonetheless, if agreement can be reached earlier on reasonably specific and detailed goals, they may be used to guide the initial work of the process, to facilitate the framing of strategic issues, or to direct strategy formulation efforts. Similarly, a vision of success typically is developed toward the end of the process, to guide implementation, but under certain circumstances it may be prepared earlier. Like the activities to formulate goals, visioning activities can be used to guide the planning process from the beginning or to frame strategic issues; they can also help in the development of strategies.

Key Design Choices

A number of interconnected design choices must be made to enhance the prospects for a successful strategic planning process. These choices are some of the most important decisions organizations make when it comes to strategic planning. Key among these important choices are the following:

- Whose plan is it?

    Is the plan to be "owned" by a community, collaboration, organization, organizational unit, program, project, or function?

    What are the implications of this choice for participation?

- What are the purposes of the strategic planning effort?

    In what ways are the planning process and the plan intended to enhance organizational or community performance and create public value?

    What other benefits of strategic planning are sought?

    What values should the process itself embody in the way it is organized and pursued?

- How will the process be tailored to the situation at hand?

    Has strategic planning been attempted before—successfully or unsuccessfully? What conclusions or lessons should be drawn from these prior efforts?

    Are goal formulation and visioning activities necessary, and if so, where will they occur in the process?

    Which approach to the identification of strategic issues will be used?

    How will the process fit with other ongoing organizational processes and change efforts, such as budgeting cycles or process improvement and information technology initiatives?

How will the process be tailored to fit the organization's culture—even if that culture is one of the targets of change?

- How will the process be sponsored and managed?

Who will sponsor the process? Does the sponsor (or sponsors) have enough power and authority to get the process going and oversee it through to completion?

Who will manage the process on a day-to-day basis, meaning who will be the process champion(s)?

How will the process be broken down into phases, activities, and tasks?

What is the project time frame?

What kind of consultation and facilitation will be needed?

How will the process accommodate commitments from sponsors and participants in terms of time, energy, and financial and political resources?

How will the process foster ongoing learning and midcourse corrections?

- What are the requirements for success?

What should or must happen against key organizational performance indicators?

Who must be a part of any winning coalition?

What is necessary for the process to be seen as legitimate in terms of procedure, process, support, and content?

What is it about the culture that must be honored? What has to change?

What organizational competencies are required for any process to succeed?

What are the absolute minimum resource requirements, those without which the process is doomed to fail? (Recall that management attention is likely to be the most crucial resource.)

What Are the Dangers to Avoid?

There are many ways in which strategic planning can fail. Without broad and supportive sponsorship, careful and skilled management, adequate resources, excellent timing, and a fair measure of luck, the process may fail. Whenever you ask people to focus in a serious way on what is fundamental and to consider doing things differently, you threaten the organization's existing culture, coalitions, values, structures, processes, and interaction patterns. Frustration, anger (even rage), and rejection of the process may result, no matter how necessary the process may be to ensure organizational survival and prosperity.

There is also likely to be an inherent skepticism about and resistance to strategic planning among line managers, who have a strong operational orientation. They will want to know what such planning can do for them.

What Are the Keys to a Successful Process?

In many ways the keys to success are the mirror image of the potential sources of failure:

Be sure the organization is ready. Conduct a readiness assessment. There need to be good reasons for doing strategic planning. But even when there are good reasons to do it, the organization still needs to be prepared to engage in a successful process. If the organization is not prepared to do strategic planning, identify capacity problems and focus thought and action on remedying them. Use Worksheets 1 through 7 and Resource A to assist you in determining whether your organization is ready for strategic planning.

Strengthen leadership and ensure adequate participation by key stakeholders. You will need strong sponsors and the support of key stakeholders throughout the process. Include major decision makers, managers, opinion leaders, and other stakeholders essential to the success of the effort. Make sure they are willing to devote the time needed to discuss what is truly important for the organization and to act on what they learn.

Make sure the process has a skillful champion (or champions). Sponsors provide the authority and power to initiate, carry out, and legitimize the process. But sponsors are typically not involved in managing the process on a day-to-day basis—the champion is. You need a champion who understands the process and is committed to it. Note that champions are not committed to specific issues and strategies; they are committed to getting key people together to focus on what is important and to do something about it.

Build understanding to support wise strategic thinking, acting, and learning. Clearly communicate the purposes of the process to key stakeholders. Engage in the analysis, synthesis, and deliberations required to build adequate understanding of the organization, its circumstances, and its potential strategic choices. Manage expectations so that neither too much nor too little is expected of the process. Take the time and allocate the resources to "do it right."

Cultivate necessary political support. Sponsorship by key decision makers is typically crucial to the success of a strategic planning effort. Beyond that, a coalition of supporters must be built that is large enough and strong enough to adopt the strategic plan and support it during implementation.

Foster effective decision making and implementation. Help decision makers focus on the truly important issues. Develop strategies with implementation in mind.

Link the strategic plan to resource allocation decisions. Develop an implementation process and action planning efforts that will ensure the realization of adopted strategies, and link these processes to operational plans and to resource allocation decisions.

Design a process that is likely to succeed. Build on existing planning, management, and other change efforts and routines, while still keeping the strategic planning process unique and special. Fit the process to the situation at hand. Fit the process to the organization's (or collaboration's or community's) culture. Use the process to inform key decisions. Be realistic about the scope and scale of the strategic planning agenda. Find a way to accommodate the day-to-day demands on people's time. Make sure that people see the process as genuinely helpful.

Manage the process effectively. Commit the resources necessary for a successful effort. Draw on people who are skilled in the process of strategic planning.

The Functions and Purposes of Strategic Planning and Management

Figure 5 presents the final view of strategic planning. It shows how the steps of the Strategy Change Cycle are designed to help an organization fulfill five functions (or major categories of actions) important to creating desired outcomes. The overall purpose of strategic planning and management is to create public value, chiefly through helping the organization fulfill its mission and meet its mandates. Moving down the left-hand and middle chains of arrows indicates that in order to do this the organization needs to deliberatively produce fundamental decisions and actions that shape and guide what the organization is, what it does, and why it does it—the very definition of strategic planning. Effective strategic planning depends on five key, interconnected functions being performed well: organizing effective participation; creating meritorious ideas for mission, goals, strategies, actions, and other strategic interventions; building a winning coalition; effectively implementing strategies; and building capacity for ongoing implementation, learning, and change. The ten steps of the Strategy Change Cycle, other process design features, and the actions they foster are designed to help fulfill these functions and thereby help to create the desired outcomes. The specific application of the Strategy Change Cycle must be tailored to the context within which it is to be pursued. Moving up the chains of arrows indicates that the process design features and steps must be tailored to the specific context, and the process must fulfill the key functions if fundamental decisions and actions are to be produced, the mission fulfilled and mandates met, and real public value created.

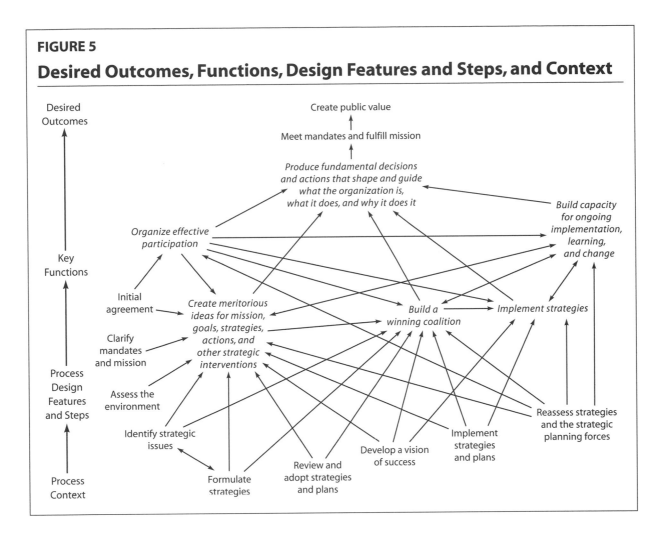

FIGURE 5

Desired Outcomes, Functions, Design Features and Steps, and Context

Readiness Assessment Directions and Worksheets

1. Someone or some group must initiate the process of readiness assessment for strategic planning. This readiness assessment person or group may not necessarily be the strategic planning process sponsor or the process champion, but the group members should be willing to explore, in a candid and constructive way, the usefulness of strategic planning for the organization or community.

2. Consider involving two kinds of stakeholders at some point in the readiness assessment process. The first group might be called *process* stakeholders—people who need to be involved in some way for the strategic planning process to be successful. They may or may not have a significant impact on the organization's issue agenda, but their involvement and support are necessary to legitimize the process of strategic planning and important to implementing

any resulting plan. The second group might be called the *agenda* stakeholders—people or organizations such as clients, customers, funders, regulators, unions, or others that have significant influence over the agenda of the organization. In general, people should be involved in the readiness assessment either because they have information or insight that cannot be gained any other way or because their support for both the process and the plan's issues is crucial. Persons may be process or agenda stakeholders for a variety of reasons: for example, the positions they hold, their reputations, or their influence or knowledge regardless of position (Bryson, 2011). Some interviewing may be necessary to explore who the readiness assessment participants should be, what issues might arise as a result of engaging in strategic planning, and what people's hopes and fears for the process might be. Use Worksheet 1 as a guide for the interviews.

3. After the readiness assessment participants have been selected, have them work individually to fill out Worksheets 2 through 5, and then have them discuss their responses as a group. In order to gain a broader perspective, the readiness assessment group might also consider conducting a broader survey of internal and external stakeholders, using the Model Readiness Assessment Questionnaire in Resource A or the questionnaires in Resources F and G, or you may consider using these questionnaires in Step 4 (assessing the environment to identify strengths, weaknesses, opportunities, and challenges).

4. Next the readiness assessment group should fill out Worksheet 6, basing this activity on the results of the discussion of Worksheets 2 through 5, perhaps as informed by the Readiness Assessment Questionnaire responses. Then, working with the responses and discussion recorded in Worksheet 6, the group should develop recommendations for the organization's leadership team and perhaps other key stakeholders about whether and how to go about strategic planning. (In small organizations, the assessment participants are likely to be the leadership team.) These recommendations should include advice about how to approach the first formal step in the process, the initial agreement step. In other words, the initial agreement step actually consists typically of a series of agreements involving increasingly wider circles of participants; the first of these agreements is embodied in the recommendations of the readiness assessment group to the organization's leadership.

5. Have the organization's leadership, along with the readiness assessment participants, fill out Worksheet 7 and discuss the results and implications for the organization and the process of strategic planning.

6. Decide as an organization whether it makes sense to

   a. Move forward on organization-wide strategic planning at this time, and, if so, how.

   b. Address a narrower agenda of key organizational process or capacity issues first.

   c. Wait for a more propitious time.

Strategic planning will require significant organizational leadership, effort, commitment, and resources if it is to be done successfully, so the decision of whether or not to undertake a strategic planning process and when to do it is a significant one.

WORKSHEET 1

Interviewing People About the Proposed Strategic Planning Process

Instructions. Those thinking about undertaking a strategic planning process should consider interviewing key decision makers and other internal and external stakeholders first about prior strategic planning efforts and reasons why a new effort might be pursued. The interviews may be very helpful in building support for strategic planning and making sure the process is designed in such a way that it will be most useful.

Consider interviewing those who might have an interest in sponsoring, championing, or otherwise leading the effort; and those who would most affect or be affected by the effort. Group interviews may also be useful but will need to be effectively facilitated, and an adequate record must be kept of ideas offered and conclusions reached. Group interviews can be a part of a targeted outreach and communications program designed to build support for a strategic planning process.

Some preliminary stakeholder analysis may be necessary in order to develop the appropriate list of people or groups to be interviewed. After the interviewees have been selected, those exploring the worth of a strategic planning process should do the interviewing. It may be wise to have two interviewers conduct each interview—to gain a clearer understanding of what is being said and not said, to improve note-taking accuracy, and to broaden identification of the implications for planning process design.

Consider using the following list of questions as a guide. Ask the person being interviewed to answer the questions from his or her own perspective, not from that of the organization as a whole. To promote candor, emphasize that all interviews will be kept confidential. To promote participation, note that summary information will be made available in the future.

Interview Prior to Readiness Assessment for Strategic Planning

Date: _____

Name of interviewer(s): _____

Interviewee's (or group's) name: _____

Organization unit: _____ Function: _____

Personnel classification: _____

Contact information: _____

External stakeholder name: _____ Title: _____

Contact information: _____

1. What do you think the most important reasons are for undertaking a strategic planning effort? Why do you think so?

Reasons for Engaging in Strategic Planning	Can You Say More About That?

Worksheet 1

Creating Your Strategic Plan, Third Edition.

2. What are the major substantive and process issues that need to be addressed as part of the process?

Substantive Issues (for example, need to improve client satisfaction, need to address funding shortages, and so forth)	Process Issues (for example, need to ensure adequate participation, need for reasonable transparency, need to improve quality of decision making, and so forth)

Worksheet 1

Creating Your Strategic Plan, Third Edition.

3. What are the 5 priority issues that you think should be addressed first? Please rank them from 1 to 5, with 1 being the most important.

   (1)

   (2)

   (3)

   (4)

   (5)

4. What do you think needs to stay the same or endure as a result of the strategic planning process, and what should change?

Stay the Same	Change

5. Who should have a role in the strategic planning process and why? Who should probably not have a role in the process and why?

Should Have Some Role	Should Probably Not Have a Role

6. For the strategic planning efforts to succeed, what do you think must happen? In other words, what do you think is absolutely necessary for success? Why do you think so?

Required for Strategic Planning Success	Why Is It a Requirement?

Worksheet 1

7. Can you think of any key questions that we have not touched on?

8. Do you have any other insights, ideas, or suggestions regarding strategic planning for this organization?

Thank you for your time!

Worksheet 1

WORKSHEET 2

Strengths, Weaknesses, Opportunities, and Challenges (or Threats)

Instructions. The *readiness* or capacity of an organization to undertake a strategic planning process successfully should be clearly understood by the organization and its leaders before the process is begun. Organizational barriers to success should be identified and evaluated, and a plan or strategy should be developed to address them (see Worksheet 3).

The following organizational areas should be explored through interviews, focus groups, or the use of tailored questionnaires: mission and vision; budget, human resources, and information technology; communications; leadership, management, organizational structure and design, and culture.

I. Mission and Vision

Successful organizations possess a clear understanding of their mandates, and they have established and communicated an inspiring organizational mission and/or vision to their stakeholders.

_____

Please comment below on any significant organizational strengths, weaknesses, opportunities, and challenges (or threats) in the areas of mission and vision. (Use additional space as necessary.)

Examples:

- We have too many mandates. (A weakness or a challenge, or both)
- Our current mission statement is an effective statement of organizational purpose. (A strength)

II. Budget, Human Resources, and Information Technology

Successful organizations and managers achieve their mandates, fulfill their mission, and create public value by effectively managing their resources.

Please comment below on any significant organizational strengths, weaknesses, opportunities, or challenges (or threats) in the areas of budget, human resources, and information technology. (Use additional space as necessary.)

Examples:

- We are short-handed in several key areas of operation (or certain skill sets, specific units, or particular substantive areas, and the like). (A weakness or a challenge, or both)

- How do we find the time to engage in an effective strategic planning effort? (A challenge)

- We have the technology we need to do our work. (A strength)

- We do not appear to have the resources we need to do a good job of strategic planning and especially of implementation. (A possible weakness or a challenge, or both)

III. Communications

Successful organizations transmit clear messages, have well-developed communication networks, and have adequate forums to promote discussion, dialogue, and shared understanding. *Messages* are concise, they are targeted toward specific stakeholders, and are designed to produce specific responses. *Networks* effectively convey appropriate information to targeted stakeholders, both internal and external. *Forums* engage appropriate stakeholders in appropriate ways to foster necessary discussion and dialogue.

Please comment on any significant organizational strengths, weaknesses, opportunities, or challenges in the area of communications.

Examples:

• Internal communications related to human resources are effective. (A strength)

• External communications with some important funders are fragmented and unfocused. (A weakness)

• There are technology-poor areas in our organization. (A challenge)

IV. Leadership, Management, Organizational Structure, and Culture

Successful organizations enjoy effective leadership and competent management and organize themselves strategically. *Leadership* means making sure that the organization is doing the right things. *Management* means making sure that those things are being done right. The *organizational structure and design* should have well-defined groupings and relationships horizontally and vertically, formally and informally, which will help it carry out specific strategic initiatives. The organization's *culture* and *values* should foster a commitment to fulfilling the mission, meeting the mandates, creating public value, and satisfying key stakeholders.

Please comment on any significant organizational strengths, weaknesses, opportunities, or challenges in the areas of leadership, management, organization, and culture.

Examples:

- The organization's top leaders are committed to strategic planning. (A strength)

- Middle management is not committed to strategic planning. (A weakness)

- Our organization's formal structure is antiquated given our mission. (A challenge)

- We do not reward risk taking and indeed punish entrepreneurial behavior. (A weakness)

WORKSHEET 3

Barriers to Strategic Planning

Instructions. On the basis of information learned from Worksheets 1 and 2, what do you see as the major internal and external barriers to a successful strategic planning process? (*Examples:* internal lack of leadership, communication problems with external audiences, resources to fund basic operations.) How can these barriers be addressed?

Internal Barriers	Ways the Barriers May Be Addressed

External Barriers	Ways the Barriers May Be Addressed

WORKSHEET 4

Expected Costs of Strategic Planning

Instructions.

1. List the financial and other costs (direct or indirect, or both) you expect to incur from strategic planning. (*Examples:* financial and staff resources required to implement the process and plan; time required; organizational conflicts and resistance to change; other stakeholder resistance.) Name the most important of these.

2. Note some ways to manage these costs.

Financial and Other Costs (direct or indirect, or both)	Ways to Manage Costs

WORKSHEET 5

Expected Benefits of Strategic Planning

Instructions.

1. List the benefits, direct and indirect, you expect from strategic planning. (*Examples:* better use of the organization's resources, better relations with stakeholders and clients, a good plan for change and change management, greater clarity about the mission.) Note the most important of these.

2. List ways to enhance these benefits.

Benefits	Ways to Enhance Benefits

WORKSHEET 6

Thinking Strategically About Strategic Planning

Instructions. The readiness or capacity of an organization to engage successfully in a deliberative, reasonably disciplined strategic planning process should be clearly understood by the organization's leadership, and perhaps other key stakeholders, before a formal strategic planning process is begun.

Our experience has been that the most successful strategic planning efforts have occurred when the following statements have been explored as part of a readiness assessment. The readiness assessment participants should be prepared to respond with yes or no and to comment on these key statements as individuals, and then be ready to discuss the statements and answers as a group on behalf of the organization. These discussions and their results are meant to help create a good foundation for the strategic planning process. The group's deliberations should provide insight into some of the strategic issues that need to be addressed, and also should help the group develop design options for a strategic planning process that is likely to succeed because it meets all the necessary requirements for success.

---

1. We know, or can know, what our formal and informal mandates are, and have, or can have, an inspiring organizational mission.

   a. We have, or can have, a clear understanding of our formal and informal mandates.

      ❑ Yes

      ❑ No

      Comments:

   b. We have, or can have, an inspiring organizational mission.

      ❑ Yes

      ❑ No

      Comments:

2. We know, or can know, who our key and other stakeholders are, and how they relate to one another and to us.

   ❑ Yes

   ❑ No

   Comments:

3. We have, or can develop, a clear understanding of our organization's strengths, weaknesses, opportunities, and challenges (or threats).

   ❑ Yes

   ❑ No

   Comments:

   a. At this starting point, we believe our organization's strengths, weaknesses, opportunities, and challenges (or threats) are as follows:

      • Strengths:

      • Weaknesses:

      • Opportunities:

      • Challenges (or threats):

4. We understand, or can understand, our organization's culture and values.

   ❏ Yes

   ❏ No

      Comments:

5. We have established, or can establish, a clear statement of the need for or desirability of strategic planning.

   a. We have identified the urgency or desirability of acting.

      ❏ Yes

      ❏ No

         Comments:

   b. We have communicated, or can communicate, the case for action to key internal and external stakeholders.

      ❏ Yes

      ❏ No

         Comments:

6. There are, or can be, powerful sponsors of a strategic planning effort.

   ❏ Yes

   ❏ No

      Comments:

7. There is, or can be, an effective process champion to manage the strategic planning effort on a day-to-day basis.

❑ Yes

❑ No

Comments:

8. There is, or can be, an effective team to lead the planning effort.

a. We have, or can identify, a team that has, or will have, the backing of the organization's leadership to spearhead the effort.

❑ Yes

❑ No

Comments:

b. The team can access appropriate and necessary analyses and resources to support the process.

❑ Yes

❑ No

Comments:

c. The team can develop processes to include (as appropriate) both internal and external stakeholders.

❑ Yes

❑ No

Comments:

9. We have, or can have, effective forums in various parts of the organization and with outside stakeholders to promote deliberation, learning, and informed decision making as part of the strategic planning process.

   ❏ Yes

   ❏ No

      Comments:

10. We consistently learn, or can learn how to learn, in formal and informal ways from our successes and failures. We know why things work well and why they do not; and if we do not know, we can be committed to figuring out how to find out.

    ❏ Yes

    ❏ No

       Comments:

11. We have, or can develop, a process to create a clear direction and a sense of vision for the organization.

    a. We will be able to say where the organization wants to be in the future.

       ❏ Yes

       ❏ No

          Comments:

b. We can develop specific strategies and actions designed to address the issues that we face in order to get where we want to be.

❑ Yes

❑ No

    Comments:

c. We can develop the coalition of support that we need to both create a strategic plan and to implement it.

❑ Yes

❑ No

    Comments:

d. We will be able to develop adequate funding for our anticipated key strategies.

❑ Yes

❑ No

    Comments:

12. We have, or can develop, an effective communications plan for the strategic planning process.

❑ Yes

❑ No

    Comments:

13. We are prepared to plan for short-term wins and long-term gains.

    a. We can plan for short-term wins that demonstrate progress and action and can lead to long-term gains.

        ❏ Yes

        ❏ No

        Comments:

    b. We can recognize and reward those involved in the strategic planning process and its improvements.

        ❏ Yes

        ❏ No

        Comments:

    c. We can anticipate resistance to change and work to address it.

        ❏ Yes

        ❏ No

        Comments:

14. We can consolidate, or develop the capacity to consolidate, improvements in mission, mandates, systems, structures, policies, and procedures that come out of the planning process.

   a. We can keep the change process moving ahead beyond the formal strategic planning process.

   ❑ Yes

   ❑ No

   Comments:

   b. We can promote and develop people who can help to manage ongoing change as part of the strategic planning process and beyond it.

   ❑ Yes

   ❑ No

   Comments:

15. We can use the strategic planning process and strategic plan to institutionalize new approaches to ongoing organizational development.

   a. We can formally adopt the strategic planning change agenda to ensure that it is embraced by the organization and key stakeholders.

   ❑ Yes

   ❑ No

   Comments:

b. We can develop the organization's leadership development agenda around the strategic plan.

❑ Yes

❑ No

Comments:

c. We can develop incentives and human resource plans and procedures around the strategic plan.

❑ Yes

❑ No

Comments:

d. We can develop our budgets and resource expenditures around the strategic plan.

❑ Yes

❑ No

Comments:

e. We can develop our information technology budgets and processes around the strategic plan.

❑ Yes

❑ No

Comments:

f. We can develop our processes and procedures for stakeholder involvement around the strategic plan.

❑ Yes

❑ No

Comments:

16. Given the responses to and comments on these statements, we should

❑ Proceed with strategic planning.

❑ Figure out if and how to change each No answer to Yes.

❑ Forget about strategic planning for now.

Comments:

WORKSHEET 7

Should We Proceed with the Strategic Planning Process?

Instructions. Review your answers to Worksheets 1 through 6, and determine whether the following readiness criteria have been met. Then discuss your results, and decide what to do next.

	Was the Criterion Met?		
	Yes	**Partially**	**No**
Readiness criteria			
One or more strong process sponsors has agreed to serve.			
One or more strong process champions has agreed to serve.			
The process is within our mandate—or can be.			
Resources are available to do the planning.			
Resources are likely to be available to implement the plan.			
The process and the plan will be linked to our budgets and operational plans.			
The benefits outweigh the costs; the process will create real value for our organization and our stakeholders.			
Strategic planning is the right tool for what we need to do.			
We can figure out ways to deal with or mitigate any No responses to the previous criteria.			
Now is the right time to initiate the process.			
Based on our responses so far, we should			
• Proceed.			
• Figure out how to change each No to Yes.			
• Forget about strategic planning for now.			

Comments:

Part 2

Creating and Implementing Strategic Planning

Ten Key Steps

Initiate and Agree on a Strategic Planning Process

Purpose of Step

The purpose of Step 1 is to develop an initial agreement among key decision makers and opinion leaders about the overall strategic planning effort and main planning tasks and to authorize advocates and facilitators to move forward with the process. Certain external decision makers and opinion leaders may need to be parties to the agreement if their information or support will be essential to the success of the effort. This agreement represents a plan for planning—or a specific *process design*—intended to organize and guide efforts aimed at the ultimate end of creating significant and enduring public value.

This initial agreement is one of the most important steps in the whole strategic planning process. It is in Step 1 that many of the understandings and commitments necessary to produce a good process and plan are developed. Among other things, these commitments define the individuals and groups that will be relied on to carry the process forward. In addition, many critical questions concerning process design are answered. For example:

- Whose plan is it?
- What are the purposes of the process and plan?
- What are the requirements for success?
- How will the process be tailored to fit the situation?
- How will the process be managed?
- How will the process be broken down into phases or tasks?
- What schedule will be adopted?

Adequate commitments and wise process design choices are critical to a successful outcome. The worksheets at the end of this step can guide you in making these commitments and choices.

Four key roles, or functions, must be played if the strategic planning effort is to succeed:

Strategic planning process sponsor(s) (SPS)

Strategic planning process champion(s) (SPC)

Strategic planning coordinating committee (SPCC)

Strategic planning team (SPT)

Two of these roles are typically played by individuals and two by groups. These functions or roles are discussed further in the following sections.

Collectively, the roles and functions help to ensure adequate authority and power to legitimize, fund, and protect implementation efforts; the managerial capacity to oversee day-to-day implementation activity; the ability to handle cross-boundary coordination issues that are essentially strategic rather than operational; and the teamwork necessary to do the heavy lifting around developing detailed, context-specific implementation recommendations and taking necessary implementation actions.

Strategic Planning Process Sponsor

The strategic planning process sponsor (SPS) must have enough status, power, and authority to commit the organization to strategic planning and to hold people accountable for doing it well. A planning effort may have one or several sponsors. SPSs are typically top positional leaders—and often are the members of a policy board, cabinet, or executive committee acting collectively. They recognize or establish important features of the planning context, make choices and commit resources that improve the chances for success, and pay careful attention to progress along the way. They have a vested interest in achieving success and do what they can to make it happen. They also are typically important sources of knowledge about key issues and effective ways of addressing them and about the organization and its environment in general. They are likely to be especially knowledgeable about how to fit strategic planning efforts to key decision points.

SPSs should be able to do the following (or even have the following job description):

1. Articulate the purpose and importance of the effort.

2. Commit necessary resources—time, money, energy, legitimacy—to the effort.

3. Emphasize throughout the process what the results are and will be that are important to the organization's mission, mandates, and key stakeholders, and what public value will be and is being created.

4. Encourage and reward hard work, smart and creative thinking, constructive dialogue, and multiple sources of input and insight aimed at assuring successful implementation.

5. Be aware of the possible need for outside consultants.

6. Be willing to exercise power and authority to keep the process on track.

Strategic Planning Process Champion

Strategic planning process champions (SPCs) are persons appointed by the SPSs to lead the implementation effort. An SPC has the primary responsibility for managing planning effort on a day-to-day basis. SPCs are the ones who keep people on course, keep track of progress, and also pay attention to all the details. They model the kinds of behavior they hope to get from other participants: reasoned, diligent, committed, enthusiastic, and good-spirited pursuit of the common good. They push, encourage, and coach implementers and other key participants through any difficulties. SPCs need strong interpersonal skills, a commitment to getting the work done, and a good feel for how to manage complexity within the culture of the organization.

SPCs should have the following job description:

1. Keep strategic planning high on people's agendas.

2. Be committed to a successful process, not to any particular solutions to strategic issues.

3. Think about what has to come together (people, information, resources, completed work) at or before key decision points.

4. Keep rallying participants and pushing the process along.

5. Develop process and agenda champions throughout the organization.

6. Be sensitive to power differences and able to engage all implementers and find ways to share power in order to increase the chances of planning success.

Strategic Planning Coordinating Committee

If the organization is large, many people need to be involved, and the situation is complex, then a strategic planning coordinating committee (SPCC), or task force, should probably be appointed. But keep in mind that there is a difference between giving people a seat on a committee and consulting with them as part of the process. The gains from involving particular people may be available without actually appointing these people to the SPCC. Unless membership in the committee is limited, it may become too large to be effective. If an organization is the focus of attention, the SPCC typically should include a cross-section of organizational members by level and function and perhaps representatives of key external stakeholder groups as well. That said, the group probably should number no more than nine members. If necessary, the SPCC may have a large representative and legitimizing body and also a small executive committee that engages in the most extensive discussions and makes recommendations to the larger group. For a collaboration or community, a large, representative legitimizing body could coordinate the process and smaller representative bodies could attend to specific issue areas.

The SPCC should have a charter that includes at least the following responsibilities:

1. Serve as a forum for deliberation, consultation, negotiation, problem solving, or buffering among organizations, units, groups, or persons involved in the strategic planning process.

2. Ensure that all members allocate the quality time necessary to help the SPCC do its job effectively.

3. Where appropriate, approve recommendations and decisions made by the strategic planning team or serve as an advisory body to formal decision makers or policymaking bodies on strategic planning issues.

4. Record all decisions or recommendations in writing and circulate them to key stakeholder groups.

5. Rotate members to keep new ideas flowing and to widen involvement in the process if the group is to be a standing committee overseeing annual or periodic strategic planning efforts.

Strategic Planning Team

The strategic planning team (SPT) is charged with developing recommendations for key decision makers regarding strategic planning and the strategic plan. The SPT can facilitate, connect, and coordinate structures, processes, resources, or activities across organizational boundaries in ways required for successful strategic plan preparation and adoption. SPT members are selected by the SPS in consultation with the SPC and SPCC, although it is also advisable to seek advice from the rest of the organization and selected external stakeholders, as our experience shows that such broadly based advice is very helpful in getting buy-in and support for the strategic planning process.

The SPT should be able to do the following and perhaps have these responsibilities included in a formal charter:

1. Focus collective attention across all types of boundaries on strategic planning tasks, responsibilities, progress, and needed further action.

2. Help with coordinating the planning process and tasks across boundaries.

3. Make recommendations to the organization's leadership on strategic planning concerns and actions.

4. Rally key participants, and push the planning process along.

5. Provide a venue in which power is shared.

6. Offer a setting in which important conflicts may be explored and managed effectively.

7. Provide occasions for the development of strategic planning champions throughout the organization.

Possible Desired Planning Outcomes

- Agreement on the purpose, worth, and scope of the strategic planning effort.

- Agreement on the organizations, units, groups, or persons who should be involved or informed. (This requires being clear about whether the planning effort is strictly an internal process or whether it will also involve external stakeholders.)

- Identification of process phases, specific tasks, activities, and schedule.

- Identification of the form and timing of reports.

- Formation of a strategic planning coordinating committee (SPCC) that sets process policy and direction.

- Formation of a strategic planning team (SPT) that coordinates day-to-day process and plan activities and needs.

- Selection, if necessary, of a consultant team of independent process and planning experts who can help to design and facilitate the process.

- Probably, identification of the requirements for success of the process.

- Commitment of necessary resources to begin the effort, and indications that resources necessary for implementation may be found.

Worksheet Directions

Locate a person or group in your organization (collaboration or community) who is willing and able to act as the *initial process champion*—that is, the person who will initiate early efforts on behalf of the process and act as an advocate for the strategic planning effort. This person must be seen as a desirable, respected, and legitimate choice by those who will be involved in the process. The initiator may not be the ultimate process champion, but he or she has enough enthusiasm, cachet, and interest to get the process going early on.

The first three items in the following directions will help you to make the best use of Worksheet 8.

1. Clearly identify *whose* plan this is. Consider the following questions from the very beginning, and ask the SPT and SPCC as well once they have been formed:

    Who are the process sponsor (or sponsors) and the process champion (or champions)?

    What part of the organization (or collaboration or community) is the plan for? And is it needed? (*Example:* A plan may be a single strategic plan for your whole organization, or it may be a division or department plan for management only. Both are legitimate if they can address the issues and meet the objectives and expectations.)

    Who will support the plan?

2. Make sure that the time frames for the plan and the process are realistic. If they are too long, the plan and the process will not be relevant; if they are too short, the plan may not be strategic enough and is unlikely to have the necessary support. A two- to five-year plan horizon and a six- to twelve-month strategic planning process may be reasonable in many cases. Ask your team:

    What information is currently available to us, and how valid and reliable is it?

    What information do we need to generate, and how valid and reliable must it be?

    What issues are driving planning needs? Are they long term (for example, matters of capital budgeting or major information technology investments) or short term (for example, operational issues)?

    How rapidly are changes occurring, and what will the time frame of the plan be?

    How do we get the most value from the process?

    What are the key requirements for success (for example, leadership commitment, key stakeholder support, new resources, reorganized work processes)?

3. In planning the process:

    Don't underestimate the level of effort and the time required to do the job well. That does not mean that the process has to drag on, but you need to allow enough time for adequate information gathering, discussion and dialogue, deliberation and decision making, and follow-through.

Match the time to the purpose, the process, the necessary involvements of people in the process, and the requirements for success.

Allow adequate time, or don't do a strategic plan.

As one of its first tasks, the SPCC should draft a strategic planning process *charter* to which process sponsors, champions, and participants agree. The charter should be drafted in light of the understandings and agreements worked out in response to Worksheet 8. The charter should be short, and at an absolute minimum, should describe the purpose of the process.

4. Use Worksheet 9 to help identify and clarify the SPT's membership, roles and responsibilities, time frame of operation, and reporting relationships, along with any needed or desirable subgroups of the SPT. Note that subgroups may include people who are not official members of the SPT.

5. Have the SPCC and SPT use Worksheet 10 to guide their meetings.

6. Have the SPCC and SPT use Worksheet 11 to summarize their meetings and assign responsibilities for next steps.

7. The SPCC and SPT should use Worksheet 12 to evaluate and improve meeting effectiveness.

8. Worksheet 13 can help the SPCC and SPT (and other involved groups) to turn their meetings into important forums for fostering learning.

9. The SPS, SPC, SPCC, and SPT should jointly use Worksheet 14 to design an effective communications plan to support the strategic planning effort.

10. The SPS, SPC, SPCC, and SPT should use Worksheet 15 in developing an effective *elevator speech* for team members and others to use to communicate the purpose and worth of the strategic planning effort.

WORKSHEET 8

Plan the Planning Effort

1. Whose plan is it? (This question is key in determining the scope of the plan and who needs to be involved in the process. You might create an initial strategic planning team to develop a draft *charter* statement as a way to explore this question.)

The plan is for (you may check more than one):

❑ The whole organization

❑ The whole organization, with separate plans for major divisions, units, and so forth

❑ Part of the organization (specify the division, unit, or program):

❑ A business, human resource, or information technology function (specify):

❑ Strictly internal stakeholders, or will also involve external stakeholders (specify):

❑ A collaboration (specify members or potential members, including whether governments, nonprofits, or businesses are involved):

❑ A community (specify):

2. What period of time will the plan cover? (Keep the time horizon realistic; otherwise, the credibility and usefulness of the plan will be undermined.)

❑ 2 years

❑ 5 years

❑ Other (specify):

3. What opportunities, challenges, issues, problems, or concerns do you hope the planning process and the plan itself will address? You may want to look again at the readiness assessment worksheets (1 to 7) and questionnaire (Resource A) to see if anything needs to be brought forward and addressed as part of this process.

4. Who is sponsoring the strategic planning process? And do they have the necessary authority and power and the resources and time?

   ❑ Senior managers

   ❑ Middle managers

   ❑ Policy board members

   ❑ Staff

   ❑ External stakeholders (including funders)

   ❑ Others (specify):

5. Who is the process champion(s)? (Identify as many as you have.) And does each champion have the backing of the sponsors, and does he or she have the necessary ability, resources, and time, as well as the respect of participants?

6. Who will be on the strategic planning project team?

   ❑ Policy board members

   ❑ Senior managers

   ❑ Middle managers

   ❑ Staff

   ❑ Other stakeholders, including possibly external stakeholders such as volunteers or funders

   ❑ Consultants

7. What kind and size of strategic planning team works (or will work) best in your organization? Think about who should own and be committed to the plan at the end of the process and what that means for the composition of the strategic planning team.

8. Who should be involved in the development of the plan? Again, think about who should own and be committed to the plan at the end of the process and what that means for involvement in the strategic planning effort.

9. Who should or will need to be involved in the review of the plan prior to and during any formal adoption process?

10. Who are the audiences for the plan? To whom will it be marketed?

11. What settings or forums are available for dialogue and deliberation as the planning process proceeds? Where will the strategic planning team meet? What kinds of forums are necessary for engaging others in the strategic planning process, and where and how might they be held?

12. How many hours are you willing to give to the strategic planning process, including meetings?

    ❑ 1–12

    ❑ 12–24

    ❑ 24–40

    ❑ 40+

13. Are you using internal or external consultants or other resource experts (such as group process facilitators, content experts, survey research firms, or communications experts)?

    ❑ Yes. Who will they be and what roles will they play?

    ❑ No

    ❑ Unsure. If you are unsure, what kind of help do you think you might need?

14. How will you coordinate with and use consultants and process experts?

15. Who other than the champion will provide administrative support for the day-to-day work of planning effort?

16. What type of written plan do you envision?

❑ Short executive summary

❑ Longer and more detailed but not including most tactical and operational elements

❑ A detailed plan that includes tactical and operational elements

❑ Other (specify):

17. What is the expected time frame for the planning process?

❑ 6 months

❑ 12 months

❑ Other (specify):

18. What steps will you use in your planning process? Review these steps with the people who are to be involved, and refine them as needed. (We have found that project management software is an excellent tool for project planning and tracking; also see Exhibit 1.)

Steps/Tasks	Persons/Groups Involved	Schedule

19. What resources do you need to start and to complete the effort, and where will you get them?

    ❑ Budget

    ❑ People

    ❑ Information

    ❑ Facilities for meetings

    ❑ Consultants

    ❑ Volunteers

    ❑ Other (specify):

20. Once those involved in the planning have created politically acceptable, administratively and technically feasible, and legal and ethical strategies designed to address the key strategic issues, are key stakeholders likely to be willing to implement them (assuming reasonable education and preparation), even if they require the organization (or collaboration or community) to look at or do things quite differently from the way they are being done now?

    ❑ Yes, with the following caveats:

    ❑ No, for these reasons:

    ❑ Unsure. If you are unsure, what additional information do you need?

21. What criteria do you think should be used to judge the effectiveness of the strategic planning *process*?

22. What criteria do you think should be used to judge the effectiveness of the strategic *plan*?

Strategic Planning Team Membership, Roles and Responsibilities, Reporting Relationships, Tasks, and Competencies

Strategic Planning Team

Members	Team Roles and Responsibilities	Starting and Ending Dates of Assignment	Team Reporting Relationships for the Strategic Planning Process

SPT Subgroups	Charge/Task	Membership (not all subgroup members need to be official SPT members)	Each Member's Knowledge Base and Competencies	Roles and Responsibilities	Starting and Ending Dates for Assignment	Reporting Relationships for the Task
Subgroup A						
Subgroup B						
Subgroup C						

Worksheet 9

Creating Your Strategic Plan, Third Edition. Copyright © 2011 by John Wiley & Sons, Inc. All rights reserved.

WORKSHEET 10

Meeting Agenda

Members present (and absent): _____

Date: _____   Time: Start _____   End _____

Place of meeting: _____

Premeeting preparation (what to read, research, or prepare):

_____

_____

_____

Time	Topic/Task	Person Responsible	Objective and Expected Outcome (what the group is to know/ discuss/create as a result)

Date of next meeting: _____

WORKSHEET 11

Meeting Summary

Date: _____

Meeting facilitator: _____   Recorder: _____

Attendees: _____

_____

_____

Action taken/decisions made:

1.

2.

3.

Notes regarding key points:

Actions to Be Taken	Person Responsible	Expected Completion Date
Summarize meeting/distribute minutes		
Gather information/research a topic		
Report to/brief someone/write briefing		
Seek input from someone		
Invite resource person(s) to future meeting		
Implement decision		
Update team work plan		

Next meeting date: _____

Worksheet 11

Creating Your Strategic Plan, Third Edition.

WORKSHEET 12

Meeting Evaluation

Instructions. Meetings can be evaluated by the team leader, a visitor to the team, or by the team members. All can contribute to improving a meeting.

Meeting Evaluation by Team Members Responding Individually

1. To what extent did this meeting achieve the stated objectives?

   Not at All   1   2   3   4   5   Completely

2. What was most helpful to you in advancing the work of the team?

3. What aspects were least helpful to you in advancing the work of the team?

4. Suggestions for improvement or other comments:

Meeting Evaluation by Team Members in a Group Discussion

1. How did we do in meeting our objectives for this meeting?

2. What can be done to improve our work together?

WORKSHEET 13

Designing Learning Forums

Instructions. Learning forums are needed wherever it is important to examine information and explore its meaning and significance as a prelude to deciding what present or future action might be needed. Learning forums have the following characteristics (D. P. Moynihan, *The Dynamics of Performance Management* [Washington, DC: Georgetown University Press, 2008], p. 179).

- They are routine and not extraordinary events and processes.

- Confrontations are avoided so as not to trigger defensive reactions.

- A collegial environment is established in which status and power differences are minimized.

- Participants include a diverse set of actors responsible for producing useful knowledge and recommendations.

- Dialogue is the norm and the dialogue is focused on how to discern and achieve organizational goals, meet the mandates, and fulfill the mission.

- Assumptions are identified and closely examined, perhaps even suspended for the sake of argument.

- Quantitative information and knowledge are used to the extent possible, including information and knowledge related to goals, issues, outputs, outcomes, strengths and weaknesses, comparisons and contrasts, and baselines.

- Experiential knowledge about how things are working (or not) is welcomed.

  Note that meetings of standing groups can be learning forums, as when school boards alternate study sessions (learning forums) with decision-making sessions.

Answer the following questions:

1. At what places in the strategic planning process and levels in the organization is it necessary or desirable to have ongoing learning forums?

2. Which already existing groups can serve as learning forums for some of the work?

3. What new learning forums will be needed? What will they focus on?

4. Who will convene each group?

5. What kind of training will be needed to help each group embody the characteristics of effective learning groups?

6. What is the process by which learning will be translated into advice?

7. How will the effectiveness of learning groups be evaluated?

8. How will the work of learning groups be acknowledged and celebrated?

Strategic Planning Process Communications Plan

Instructions. Effective strategic planning depends on effective communications. Indeed, the message from successful practice is basically, "Communicate, communicate, communicate!" Complete the following chart to identify the process and schedule for reporting, who is responsible, and what the medium is.

Strategic Planning Component	Who Is Responsible for Communicating?	Schedule for Communicating (such as weekly, monthly, quarterly, yearly, on an as-needed basis)	Who Is the Audience (such as managers, SPCC, board, funders, external partners, general public)	Process for Communicating (such as data collection, data presentation, summaries and recommendations, requests for assistance)	Relevant Performance Indicators	Medium (such as face-to-face meeting, e-mail, Web posting, hard-copy report, annual report)
Organizing the process and analyzing the environment						
Clarifying mission, mandates, vision sketch, and values						
Assessing internal and external environments						
Identifying and analyzing strategic issues						

Strategic Planning Component	Who Is Responsible for Communicating?	Schedule for Communicating (such as weekly, monthly, quarterly, yearly, on an as-needed basis)	Who Is the Audience (such as managers, SPCC, board, funders, external partners, general public)	Process for Communicating (such as data collection, data presentation, summaries and recommendations, requests for assistance)	Relevant Performance Indicators	Medium (such as face-to-face meeting, e-mail, Web posting, hard-copy report, annual report)
Developing strategies and action plans						
Reviewing and adopting the strategic plan						
Implementing strategies						
Ongoing operations						
Other						
Other						

Comments:

WORKSHEET 15

Creating an Elevator Speech

Instructions. An important communication tool is the short speech that provides a compelling message about what the strategic planning effort is about, how the work is being done, why it is important, and for whom it matters. The message is similar to a *vision sketch* of success (see Worksheet 26), but it can be delivered in sixty seconds—all the time you might have to spend with another person. Note that the speech may be filled in and refined as the process proceeds.

Answer the following questions and then ask someone with a flair for simple, direct, vivid language to prepare the elevator speech, perhaps in bullet point form. Different formats (a brochure, a PowerPoint presentation, the organization's Web site or Facebook page, and so forth) might be used to get the message across in a variety of ways to different audiences.

1. What is being done?

2. Why is strategic planning important at this time?

3. Who will be helped (for example, staff, clients, funders) by this effort? And where are they?

4. How will they be helped?

5. Why is this important for those being helped and for the organization?

6. When is the work being done, and when are significant results expected?

The sixty-second elevator speech should include the following points:

Clarify Organizational Mandates

Purpose of Step

The purpose of Step 2 is to clarify the nature and meaning of externally imposed mandates that the organization is required to meet. Mandates may be expressed formally or informally. Formal mandates prescribe what must or should be done under the organization's current charter and policies and under federal, state, and local laws, codes, bylaws, and regulations. Informal mandates may be embodied in election results, internal culture and belief systems, or community or key stakeholder expectations.

As the organization sets its future course, planners need to take both formal and informal mandates into account as constraints on the goals the organization can achieve and the ways it can achieve them. It is vital that the organization have a clear understanding of its current mandates and of their implications for its actions and resources.

Having said this, we should point out two things: First, many mandates are as much enablers of action as they are constraints on it. Second, many organizations assume they are far more constrained than they actually are. Because some mandates enable a wider range of action than organizational members assume, what people may think is mandated may turn out not to be. Other mandates will have become dated and inappropriate. Organizational mythology as well as culture needs to be reviewed, and the real mandates need to be identified, along with mandates that should be changed.

An equally common error is to overemphasize one aspect of the organization's mandates at the expense of others. For example, some organizations have support and service responsibilities as well as regulatory oversight responsibilities. The proper balance between service and support on the one hand and control and enforcement on the other hand is often an important issue. Our experience is that usually one aspect of such responsibilities dominates the organization's culture, and so one type of mandate gets most of the attention, which may not be in either the organization's or the public's best interests.

Possible Desired Planning Outcomes

- Compilation of the organization's formal and informal mandates

- Interpretation of what is required by the mandates and what is not, including identifying what may be simply ingrained habits or ways of doing things

- Clarification of what is not ruled out by the mandates

- Evaluation of whether specific mandates are still viable and desirable or are dated and in need of change

Worksheet Directions

1. Have someone compile a list of the formal and informal mandates faced by the organization (Worksheet 16 can guide this activity).

2. Review these mandates to clarify what is required and what is allowed. Discuss the implications of the mandates for existing or potential programs, projects, and services and for resource allocations. Have individuals fill out Worksheet 17 by themselves first, to establish a basis for getting the discussion started.

3. Frame a clear, concise mandate statement, and regularly remind organizational members of what the organization is required to do. This ensures conformity with the mandates and identifies where the organization has discretionary authority and where it does not. (When a mandate is found to be an issue, it may need to be changed.)

Initial Compilation of Mandates

Instructions. Use this worksheet as a guide, but create your own organizational mandate evaluation criteria.

Mandate	Source (charter, policy, rules, law, stakeholder expectations, cultural norms, and so forth)	Key Requirements	Effects on Organization	Evaluation Criteria (check appropriate box)
				☐ Funded ☐ Still appropriate ☐ Out-of-date ☐ Conflicts with others
				☐ Funded ☐ Still appropriate ☐ Out-of-date ☐ Conflicts with others
				☐ Funded ☐ Still appropriate ☐ Out-of-date ☐ Conflicts with others
				☐ Funded ☐ Still appropriate ☐ Out-of-date ☐ Conflicts with others
				☐ Funded ☐ Still appropriate ☐ Out-of-date ☐ Conflicts with others

WORKSHEET 17

Background for Group Discussion of Mandates

Instructions. Individuals should fill out this worksheet by themselves first, to establish a basis for the group discussion to follow.

1. Discuss what is "mandated," and identify the various types of mandates the organization has. What does this mean about our purpose and nature as an organization? Which mandates can and should we change as an organization, and which ones require others (for example, the legislature or the courts) to be involved? (It may be helpful to think in terms of a two-by-two matrix, with formal and informal mandates on one axis and external and internal mandates on the other.)

2. What impacts do these mandates have on our future direction as an organization, including their implications for resource availability and use?

3. What programs, services, products, and project areas are *not* ruled out by mandates?

4. What is the relationship between our organization's current mission and its mandates? Is the mission consistent with the mandates, in conflict with them, unrelated to them, inappropriately linked with them, not taking full advantage of them, and so forth?

5. What mandates may need to be changed, eliminated, or added, and why?

Worksheet 17
Creating Your Strategic Plan, Third Edition.

Identify and Understand Stakeholders, Develop and Refine Mission and Values, and Consider Developing a Vision Sketch

Purpose of Step

The purpose of Step 3 is to help planners understand more about the organization's stakeholders, clarify the organization's mission and values, and perhaps develop a vision statement to guide the rest of the process. The key to success for public and nonprofit organizations is satisfying important stakeholders according to each stakeholder's criteria for satisfaction. Mission, values, and vision should therefore be thought about in relation to those stakeholders.

Stakeholders

A stakeholder is any person, group, or organization that can place a claim on the organization's resources, attention, or output or is affected by its output. A stakeholder analysis is the means for identifying who the organization's internal and external stakeholders are, how they evaluate the organization, how they influence the organization, what the organization needs from them, and how important they are. A stakeholder analysis is particularly useful in providing valuable information about the political situation facing the organization.

The results of a stakeholder analysis can form the basis for the development and refinement of a mission statement, and they can also help determine who should be involved in the strategic planning process. (That is why the readiness assessment in Step 1 involved some preliminary stakeholder analysis.) Whom you involve in this process and how you involve them will go a long way toward determining whose process it is in practice and how successful you are likely to be in implementing any plans that are developed. (Additional detailed advice on stakeholder analyses can be found in *Strategic Planning for Public and Nonprofit Organizations*, fourth edition [Bryson, 2011], especially Chapters Three and Four and Resource A; also see Bryson, 2004.)

Mission

In Step 3, the organization's mission is identified, developed, and refined—a process that may also include clarifying the organization's values.

A mission statement is an action-oriented formulation of the organization's purpose, which in combination with the mandates provides the organization's reason for existence. A mission statement answers this question: Ultimately, *what* are we here to do, and *why*? The mission statement should be developed in light of who the organization's stakeholders are and how the organization might create public value.

The mission statement for your organization should also define, in a broad-brush way, how the organization proposes to get from where it is to where it wants to go. The statement should be meaningful yet concise.

Values

Values underpin *how* the organization operates. If an organization wants to develop a values statement, the starting point should be the following questions: How do we want to conduct our business? How do we want to treat our key stakeholders? What do we value—in other words, what do we really *care* about? A statement of organizational values can be extremely helpful for understanding the organization's culture and the issues it faces and for developing organizational goals and strategies.

Vision

A vision statement—often called a *vision of success*—describes what the organization should look like as it successfully implements its strategies and achieves its full potential. An organization typically has to go through more than one cycle of strategic planning before it can develop an effective vision for itself. A vision of success is therefore more likely to be a guide to strategy implementation than to strategy formulation. That is why Step 8 is explicitly devoted to developing a vision of success.

Nonetheless, many organizations find it very useful to develop a *vision sketch* in Step 3, as a guide for the rest of the planning process and for the plan itself. The sketch is unlikely to be so detailed as a full-blown vision of success but can still be useful in directing participant attention in subsequent steps. For example, planners can use a vision sketch in identifying strategic issues and formulating strategies to address those issues. All that is really necessary to enhance organizational achievement is to identify a few key issues and to do something effective about them. Nonetheless, if the planning group thinks it makes sense to develop a vision sketch, the group should do so.

Possible Desired Planning Outcomes

- An inclusive list of stakeholders and an analysis of how, where, when, and why to involve them in the process (beyond the preliminary analysis done in Step 1)
- A draft mission statement
- A draft values statement
- A vision sketch

Worksheet Directions

Stakeholders

1. Have your strategic planning team brainstorm a list of stakeholders (Worksheet 18) and fill out an analysis worksheet for each (Worksheets 19 and 20). See Resource B for brainstorming guidelines.

2. Then figure out where each stakeholder should be located on a power versus interest grid (Worksheet 21). The grid arrays stakeholders in terms of their power to affect the organization and their interest in the organization's work and mission.

3. On the basis of these analyses, evaluate the involvement of stakeholders in the strategic planning process (Worksheets 22 and 23). If the planning effort is to be successful and if planned strategies are to be implemented, both the process and the plan need to involve and "speak to" key stakeholders. One important area of possible involvement for both internal and external stakeholders is development of the mission statement. Stakeholders may also need to be involved in development of the values statement and vision sketch.

Mission

1. Identify and organize any existing mission-related materials. Have the strategic planning team review the materials before filling out Worksheet 24. Have participants fill out Worksheet 24 as individuals first and then discuss the answers as a group.

2. Have one person or a small group prepare a draft mission statement. Circulate the draft to stakeholders for their comments. Expect to revisit the mission statement throughout the process.

Values

1. Consider developing an explicit statement of values that indicates how your organization wants to operate and to relate to key stakeholders. Values such as respect, trust, honesty, integrity, and teamwork are often emphasized in such statements. The values statement should articulate a code of behavior to which the organization adheres or aspires.

2. Have the planning team collect any values-related material and review and discuss it. If there is none, consider developing it through group discussions with your team and key stakeholders. The values discussion can often identify strategic issues. Fill out Worksheet 25.

3. Have one person or a small group prepare a draft values statement and then have the planning team discuss it. Circulate drafts to key stakeholders for their comments. Expect to revisit the values statement throughout the process.

Vision Sketch

1. Have the planning team collect any vision-related materials and documents. Review and discuss these, then consider developing a vision sketch through group discussions with your team and key stakeholders. Think about the organization's mission and what its basic philosophy and values, strategies, and performance criteria are or should be. Think about how the organization would look if it were creating as much public value as possible.

2. Have the planning team members or key stakeholder representatives work individually to fill out Worksheet 26. The whole group should then share and discuss everyone's answers (perhaps after having small subgroups discuss their members' individual answers first).

3. Following the discussion, request that one person or a small group prepare a draft vision sketch. Then circulate drafts to key stakeholders for their comments and make modifications as appropriate until general agreement is reached. Expect to revisit the vision sketch throughout the process and especially in Step 8. Like the mission and values statements, the sketch and any subsequent vision of success will change as the organization and the factors affecting the organization change.

WORKSHEET 18

Stakeholder Identification

Instructions. The starting place for conducting a stakeholder analysis is to list the organization's stakeholders. Be as inclusive as possible the first time around in filling out the worksheet that follows. Later you and your group might consider deciding what importance each stakeholder has in terms of his or her positive or negative impact on the organization, its strategies, and its ability to fulfill its mission, meet its mandates, and create public value. A stakeholder analysis done early in the process can help you decide who should be involved in the process and when, how, and why. Additional stakeholder analyses are likely to be needed in the issues identification, strategy formulation, plan review and adoption, and implementation steps. Some stakeholders, like unions or policy board members, may be both internal and external stakeholders. Below you can see a very general example of how Worksheet 18 might be completed for a public agency. When filling out your worksheet, be more specific than the example is about stakeholder identities—in other words, say *which* state agencies and *which* nonprofit organizations are stakeholders. Have people fill out the worksheet as individuals first, and then develop a final version by discussing and pooling everyone's responses.

Example: The figure on this page displays a very general stakeholder mapping exercise for a public agency. Be more specific when you fill out your own map on the next page.

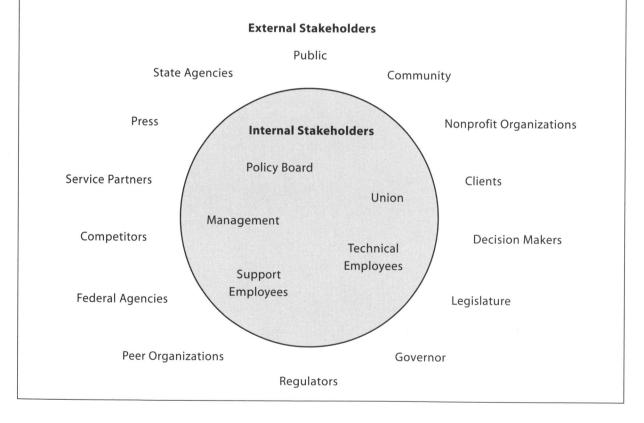

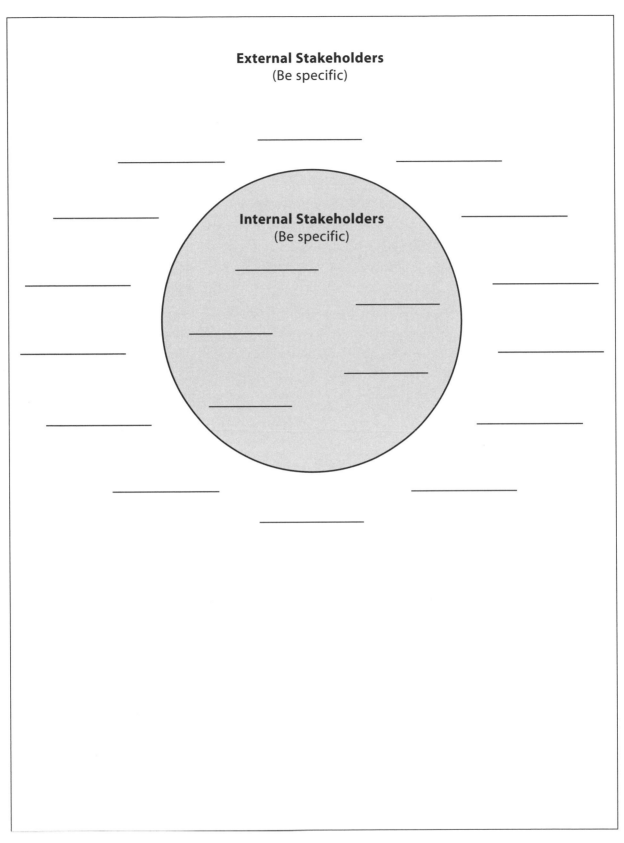

WORKSHEET 19

External Stakeholder Analysis

Instructions. An external stakeholder is any person, group, or organization outside the organization that can make a claim on the organization's attention, resources, or output or is affected by the organization's output. For example, an external stakeholder may be the organization's clients or customers for goods and services, a service partner, a funder, a regulatory entity, a union, or taxpayers and the citizenry in general.

For each external stakeholder listed on Worksheet 18, whether an individual or a group, fill out a separate External Stakeholder Analysis worksheet. Rank your stakeholders in terms of their importance to your organization and their role. In order to do the ranking, you may need to develop a set of evaluation criteria first.

Stakeholder's Name:	Type of Stakeholder		
	Client or Customer	Partner	Other

Criteria Used by Stakeholder to Assess Our Performance	Our Sense of Their Judgment About Our Performance		
	Poor	Average	Good

1. How does this stakeholder affect us, and how do we affect this stakeholder?

2. What do we need from this stakeholder, and what does this stakeholder need from us?

Worksheet 19

Creating Your Strategic Plan, Third Edition.
Copyright © 2011 by John Wiley & Sons, Inc. All rights reserved.

3. How important is this stakeholder?

☐ Extremely

☐ Reasonably

☐ Not at all

4. What role should this stakeholder have in the strategic planning process, if any?

☐ Strategic planning coordinating committee member

☐ Strategic planning team member

☐ Participant in the process

☐ Plan reviewer

☐ Decision maker

☐ Other

WORKSHEET 20

Internal Stakeholder Analysis

Instructions. An internal stakeholder is any person, group, or other entity inside the organization that can make a claim on the organization's attention, resources, or output or is affected by the organization's output. For example, internal stakeholders may be specific board members, managers, or employees, or entire groups or departments.

For each internal stakeholder individual or group listed on Worksheet 18, fill out a separate Internal Stakeholder Analysis worksheet. Rank your stakeholders in terms of their importance to your organization and their role. In order to do the ranking, you may need to develop a set of evaluation criteria first.

Stakeholder's name: _____

Criteria Used by Stakeholder to Assess Our Performance	Our Sense of Their Judgment About Our Performance		
	Poor	Average	Good

1. How does this stakeholder affect us, and how do we affect this stakeholder?

2. What do we need from this stakeholder, and what does this stakeholder need from us?

3. How important is this stakeholder?

    ☐ Extremely

    ☐ Reasonably

    ☐ Not at all

4. What role should this stakeholder have in the strategic planning process, if any?

    ☐ Strategic planning coordinating committee member

    ☐ Strategic planning team member

    ☐ Participant in the process

    ☐ Plan reviewer

    ☐ Decision maker

    ☐ Other

WORKSHEET 21

Power Versus Interest Grid

Instructions. A power versus interest grid arrays stakeholders according to two dimensions on a two-by-two matrix (often using Post-it® notes on a flipchart sheet). The dimensions are the stakeholder's interest or stake in the organization or the issue at hand, and the stakeholder's power to affect the organization or issue. *Interest* here means interest in a political sense; that is, having a political stake as opposed to simple inquisitiveness. In reality each of the dimensions is a range, from low to high interest and from low to high power, and stakeholders may be anywhere within those ranges. Nonetheless, it is often helpful to think of stakeholders as generally falling into four categories:

- *Players have both an interest and significant power.* They have a high potential to affect the strategic planning process and its outcome.

- *Subjects have an interest but little power.* It may be important to support and enhance subjects' capacity to be involved, especially when they may be affected by the planning process or its outcomes, as might be the case with program participants.

- *Context setters have power but little direct interest.* It may be important to increase the interest of context setters in the planning process or its outcomes if they are likely to pose barriers to progress through their disinterest.

- *The crowd consists of stakeholders with little interest or power.* The crowd may need to be informed about the process and its outcomes. Of course, if communication is badly done, controversy may quickly turn an amorphous crowd into a very interested mob.

Place each stakeholder name identified in Worksheets 19 and 20 in the appropriate place on the grid. As discussed, the dimensions are ranges, so that, for example, within the player category some players will be more powerful or have a stronger interest than other players. Once the stakeholders are arrayed appropriately, discuss the resulting pattern or patterns and what they mean for the organization and the strategic planning process.

Power versus interest grids typically determine which players' interests and power bases *must* be taken into account in order to produce a good strategic planning process and set of outcomes. More broadly, the grid may also highlight coalitions to be encouraged or discouraged, behavior that should be fostered, and stakeholders whose buy-in should be sought and who should be co-opted. The grid does this, in part, by revealing which stakeholders have the most to gain (or lose) and which have the most (or least) control over the direction of the process and plan. The information provides a helpful basis for assessing the political, technical, practical, and other risks as the process goes forward. (Note that Worksheet 21 relies primarily on worksheet preparers' perceptions; in some circumstances it may be necessary to gather additional information in order to be sure about relative placements of stakeholders on the grid.)

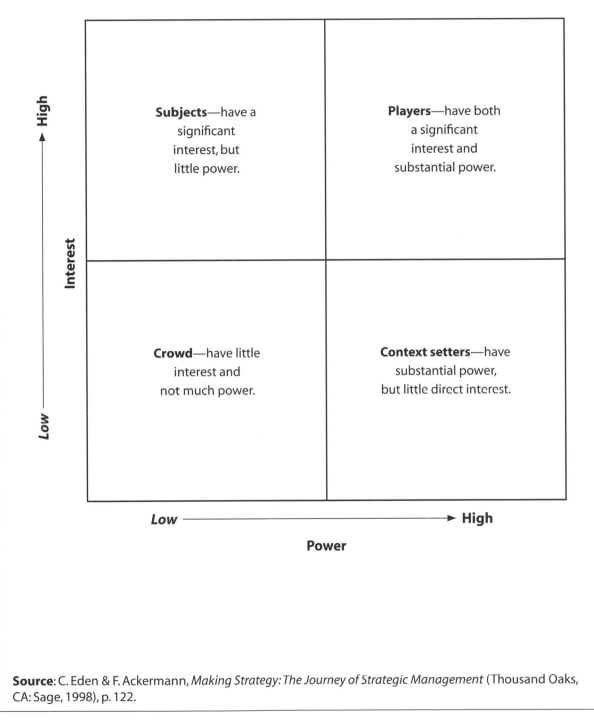

Subjects—have a significant interest, but little power.	**Players**—have both a significant interest and substantial power.
Crowd—have little interest and not much power.	**Context setters**—have substantial power, but little direct interest.

Interest: High / Low

Power: Low → High

Source: C. Eden & F. Ackermann, *Making Strategy: The Journey of Strategic Management* (Thousand Oaks, CA: Sage, 1998), p. 122.

Worksheet 21

WORKSHEET 22

Key External Stakeholder Engagement

Instructions. Identifying the organization's stakeholders is an important early—and ongoing—step in the strategic planning process. Recall that an organization's stakeholders include any person, group, or organization that can place a claim on the organization's attention, resources, or output, or is affected by that output.

Review Worksheets 18, 19, and 21 and list the key *external* stakeholders, and then decide how they should be involved in the process—or not.

Key External Stakeholder's Name	Type of Involvement					
	Ignore	Inform	Consult	Involve	Collaborate or Partner	Decision-Making Authority
		We will keep you informed of progress and results.	*We will keep you informed, listen to you, and provide feedback on how your input influenced the process.*	*We will work with you to ensure your concerns are considered and reflected in options considered, make sure you get to review and comment on options, and provide feedback on how your input is used in the process.*	*We will incorporate your advice and suggestions to the greatest extent possible and give you meaningful opportunities to be part of the decision-making process.*	*This is your strategic planning effort. We will offer options to inform your decisions. You will decide and we will support and facilitate implementing your decisions.*

Source: Some information on types of involvement adapted from International Association for Public Participation, *Spectrum of Public Participation* (http://www.iap2.org/associations/4748/files/IAP2%20Spectrum_vertical.pdf, 2007).

When you have filled out the table, revisit the question of who needs to be engaged in the strategic planning process and how. Reconsider membership of external stakeholders on the strategic planning coordinating committee, strategic planning team, and other relevant bodies. Think about how to engage key external stakeholders in other ways: for example, through focus groups, discussion groups, or surveys.

The ideal size for a strategic planning team is probably four to seven people and certainly no more than nine. The team may be a subgroup of a larger group, such as the strategic planning coordinating committee, although that group also should probably not be too large. There is a trade-off between getting many people involved and still getting some action! The point of this worksheet is to figure out how best to engage stakeholders (or not) in what ways over the course of a strategic planning process.

Having said that, we would also advise being as inclusive as possible in engaging stakeholders in other ways. Good suggestions and new ideas will come into the process, and the legitimacy of the process will be enhanced.

Keeping participants informed and appropriately engaged greatly increases ownership of the process, the plan, and its implementation. Developing an effective communications plan to keep participants informed of the strategic planning process and its progress is often very important for process and plan success.

WORKSHEET 23

Key Internal Stakeholder Engagement

Instructions. Identifying the organization's stakeholders is an important early—and ongoing—step in the strategic planning process. Recall that an organization's stakeholders include any person, group, or other entity that can place a claim on the organization's attention, resources, or output, or is affected by that output.

Review Worksheets 18, 20, and 21 and list the key *internal* stakeholders, and then decide how they should be involved in the process—or not.

Key Internal Stakeholder's Name	Type of Involvement					
	Ignore	Inform	Consult	Involve	Collaborate or Partner	Decision-Making Authority
		We will keep you informed of progress and results.	*We will keep you informed, listen to you, and provide feedback on how your input influenced the process.*	*We will work with you to ensure your concerns are considered and reflected in options considered, make sure you get to review and comment on options, and provide feedback on how your input is used in the process.*	*We will incorporate your advice and suggestions to the greatest extent possible and give you meaningful opportunities to be part of the decision-making process.*	*This is your strategic planning effort. We will offer options to inform your decisions. You will decide and we will support and facilitate implementing your decisions.*

Source: Some information on types of involvement adapted from International Association for Public Participation, *Spectrum of Public Participation* (http://www.iap2.org/associations/4748/files/IAP2%20Spectrum_vertical.pdf, 2007).

When you have filled out the table, revisit the question of who needs to be engaged in the strategic planning process and how. Reconsider membership of internal stakeholders on the strategic planning coordinating committee, strategic planning team, and other relevant bodies. Think about how to engage key internal stakeholders in other ways: for example, through focus groups, discussion groups, or surveys.

The ideal size for a strategic planning team is probably four to seven people and certainly no more than nine. The team may be a subgroup of a larger group, such as the strategic planning coordinating committee, although that group also should probably not be too large. There is a trade-off between getting many people involved and still getting some action! The point of this worksheet is to figure out how best to engage stakeholders (or not) in what ways over the course of a strategic planning process.

Having said that, we would also advise being as inclusive as possible in engaging stakeholders in other ways. Good suggestions and new ideas will come into the process, and the legitimacy of the process will be enhanced.

Keeping participants informed and appropriately engaged greatly increases ownership of the process, the plan, and its implementation. Developing an effective communications plan to keep participants informed of the strategic planning process and its progress is often very important for process and plan success.

Worksheet 23

WORKSHEET 24

Mission Statement

Instructions. A mission statement should clarify the organization's purpose and indicate why it is doing what it does. In other words, it should answer this question: Ultimately, what are we here to do, and why?

Individuals should fill out this worksheet by themselves first. After they come together again and discuss the results, a single individual or small group may be charged with coming up with a new mission statement for review by key stakeholders.

Do not be surprised if a strategic issue emerges from a discussion of the organization's mission statement.

1. What is our current mission? What does it say about who we are, what our purpose is, what business we are in, whom we serve, and how we are unique?

2. In general, what are the basic social and political needs we exist to fill? Or, what are the basic social or political problems we exist to address?

3. What is our role in filling these needs or addressing these problems? How does our organization differ from other organizations?

4. In general, what do we want to do to recognize or anticipate and respond to these needs or problems?

5. How should we respond to our key stakeholders?

6. What is our philosophy, and what are our core values?

7. Is our current mission dated, and if so, how?

8. What changes in the mission would I propose?

9. Examine the answers to the prior questions and draft a mission statement. (*Example of the mission of the Los Angeles County Department of Children and Family Services:* "The Department of Children and Family Services will, with our community partners, provide a comprehensive child protection system of prevention, preservation and permanency to ensure that children grow up safe, physically and emotionally healthy, educated and in permanent homes.")

WORKSHEET 25

Values Statement

Instructions. A values statement should articulate *how* the organization will conduct itself. The statement should answer the question, How do we want to treat others and how do we want to be treated ourselves?

Do not be surprised if a strategic issue emerges from a discussion of the organization's value system.

___

1. List what you consider to be your organization's key values *in practice* at the present time. Values may be *implicit* or *explicit*. Note that an organization's values are most obvious in *how* it does things and *with whom* it does them, not in *what* it does. Note also that the *key* values may not be *good* values. (*Examples of desirable values:* honesty, integrity, caring, trust, respect, and the like; *examples of typically undesirable values:* assuming the organization knows what's best for stakeholders, frequent toleration of backdoor or end-run decision making, talking behind people's backs, willingness to tolerate sloppy record keeping, unwillingness to explore best practices elsewhere, and so on.)

Value	Is This a Desirable or Good Value?	Or Is This an Inappropriate or Bad Value?

2. Are there any additional values you would like to see the organization adopt to guide the conduct of its business and its relationships with key stakeholders? (List them here.)

3. What conflicts are there among the values that should be addressed? (Serious conflicts may indicate a strategic issue to be dealt with later in the process.)

4. Having identified both current values (desirable as well as inappropriate) and those you would like to see adopted, place an asterisk (*) next to the eight to ten values that you think are most important for the organization to embrace.

5. Engage in a group discussion and develop a working definition for each of the five or six most important values on which most people can agree.

Value	Definition

6. Now consider how you want to reflect those top values in the strategic planning process (for example, as guides to deliberation by the SCC and SPT) and in the strategic plan (for example, as a values list, as broad statements, as criteria for selecting strategies, as part of your vision statement).

WORKSHEET 26

Vision Sketch

Instructions. A vision describes in brief what the organization should look like as it successfully implements its strategies and achieves its full potential. A vision statement answers the question, Where and what do we want to be? Or put more fully, What might we look like, or what might we ideally be in the future given expected opportunities, challenges, and anticipated action needed to get there?

Typically, an organization has to go through several cycles of strategic planning in order to develop a full-blown *vision of success*, which is one reason why vision development is Step 8 in the Strategy Change Cycle. But often it makes sense to prepare a vision sketch earlier in the process—and this preliminary vision should be revisited and perhaps revised in later steps.

Do not be surprised if a strategic issue (or more than one) emerges from a discussion of individuals' vision sketches.

We suggest that people work individually to answer the first three items and then complete their worksheets through group dialogue and deliberation.

---

1. Succinctly describe the organization as it is right now. Characterize its mission or role, people, services, organization, use of technology, resources, culture, and external legitimacy and support.

   • Mission or role

   • People

- Services

- Structure

- Processes

- Use of technology

- Resources

- Culture

- External legitimacy and support

Worksheet 26

Creating Your Strategic Plan, Third Edition.

2. Now imagine it is five (or conceivably ten) years in the future and you are a journalist reporting on your organization. What do you see in the following areas?

- Mission or role

- People

- Services

- Structure

- Processes

- Use of technology

- Resources

- Culture

- External legitimacy and support

3. If your vision sketch for the organization is out of alignment with where you think things are at present, then indicate where the major misalignments or gaps are.

   - Mission or role

   - People

   - Services

   - Structure

   - Processes

   - Use of technology

   - Resources

   - Culture

   - External legitimacy and support

4. Engage in a group discussion in which you compare and contrast each other's vision sketches.

5. Assign an individual or small group the task of drafting a vision sketch that combines the best features of the individuals' sketches along with what appear to be the group's consensus views. (*Example of the mission- or role-related "guiding vision" for the Los Angeles County Department of Children and Family Services:* "Children grow up safe, physically and emotionally healthy, educated and in permanent homes.")

6. Now consider how you want to use the vision sketch to guide the strategic planning process and how it should be reflected in the strategic plan (for example, to help identify strategic issues, to guide strategy selection, to guide implementation, and to communicate with internal and external stakeholders).

Assess the Environment to Identify Strengths, Weaknesses, Opportunities, and Challenges

Purpose of Step

In Step 4, the internal strengths and weaknesses of the organization are identified, along with the organization's external opportunities and challenges (or threats). The analysis of these four elements, known by the acronym SWOC/T, is very useful in clarifying the conditions or situations within which the organization operates. Whereas the stakeholder analysis (Step 3) provides extraordinarily useful information about the politics impinging on the organization, the SWOC/T analysis supplies a kind of overall systems view of the organization and the factors that affect it.

A SWOC/T analysis is a valuable prelude to identifying and framing strategic issues in Step 5. People often want to jump straight to strategic issues without really understanding the context of the issues. As a result, strategic issues are often not clearly identified or are misidentified, which in turn means that the strategies developed in Step 6 do not address the real issues. Solving the wrong problem is a classic mistake that a good SWOC/T analysis, in conjunction with a good stakeholder analysis, can help the organization avoid (Nutt, 2002). In addition, a SWOC/T analysis brings to the surface clues about the probable contours of effective strategies, because every successful strategy builds on strengths (and especially distinctive competencies, as described in the next paragraph) and takes advantage of opportunities while it also overcomes or minimizes the effects of weaknesses and challenges. The Organization's Highs and Lows exercise (see Exercise 1) also is very useful for revealing the contours of effective (and ineffective) approaches to changing the organization.

Exercise 1: Lessons About Successful and Unsuccessful Change Management from Reviewing the Organization's Highs and Lows

Often organizational members can learn how to pursue successful changes in their organizations by comparing and contrasting the causes of memorably positive (highs) and negative (lows) organizational events. The further back people look, the better able they are to look forward (Kouzes & Posner, 2008). Strategic planning and implementation efforts may involve both highs and lows, so understanding what characterized the highs as well as the lows can help members achieve more strategic planning and implementation highs and avoid the lows. The following exercise is patterned after one for individuals outlined in Crosby and Bryson (2005, p. 50), which in turn is based on a more elaborate charting exercise described by Kouzes and Posner (2002). The exercise consists of the following steps:

1. Reserve a room with a large wall. A room with a whiteboard that covers a whole wall is ideal. Alternatively, you might wish to cover a wall with sheets of flipchart paper taped together (two rows of eight sheets each), so that the results of the exercise can be saved intact.

2. Divide the wall into top and bottom halves by drawing a horizontal line on the whiteboard or flipchart sheets with a marker or by applying a long strip of masking tape.

3. At the right-hand end of the line, write in the current year. At the left-hand end, write in the date that is as far back in time as you wish the strategic planning team to ultimately look forward in time (typically the duration of the strategic plan as indicated in Step 1).

4. Ask group members to individually and silently brainstorm, on a sheet of scratch paper, all the organizational highs and lows they can recall that occurred within the agreed time frame. These events might include the organization's founding, arrivals or departures of key leaders, successful or unsuccessful

management of crises, particularly useful or disastrous innovations, prior strategic planning efforts, and so on. Participants should date each item and label it as a high or low.

5. Have participants transcribe their highs and lows onto half sheets of paper, one high or low per sheet (or else write them on large Post-it notes). Once this is done, a piece of tape rolled sticky side out or a small bit of self-adhesive putty is attached to the back of each sheet.

6. Have participants stick their sheets to the wall at the appropriate place on the timeline. The height of each sheet above or below the line should reflect just how high the high was or how low the low was.

7. Ask the group to identify the themes that were common to the highs, to the lows, and to both. What patterns emerge across the highs and across the lows? Are the highs and lows related to one another in any way? Probe some around the role of emotion in relation to the highs and lows. Someone should be the designated note taker for this and subsequent steps.

8. Then ask the group to further analyze the data and themes by answering these questions:

   • What is common to the highs (or subsets of highs)? What made them highs? What did we do or not do, and what was out of our control?

   • What is common to the lows (or subsets of lows)? What made them lows? What did we do or not do, and what was out of our control?

   • What lessons can we draw for successfully managing change?

   • What seems to be absolutely necessary for us if we are to manage challenges successfully?

   • What helps us manage challenges successfully, but does not seem to be absolutely necessary?

9. Identify what the organization's strategies have been in practice—what has actually happened, as opposed to what might be voiced in official pronouncements. Ask what the organization seems to be particularly good at doing; probe for ambitions and competencies and how they have been linked. Also ask what the organization does not do well; look for problems with aspirations or competencies, or both.

10. To conclude the discussion, have the group move the timeline forward an equivalent distance and discuss what group members' previous analyses might imply for the future and especially for creating and implementing the strategic plan. What themes, patterns, and strategies from the past would the group like to see projected into the future? Which would the group not like to see projected? What new themes would the group like to see?

A SWOC/T analysis can help the organization identify its *critical success factors* (CSFs). These are the things the organization must do or criteria it must meet in order to be successful in the eyes of its key stakeholders, especially those in its external environment (Johnson, Scholes, & Whittington, 2008). A SWOC/T analysis will also help the organization identify the competencies and distinctive competencies it can draw on or needs to develop in order to do well against the CSFs. *Competencies* are abilities, sets of actions, or strategies at which the organization is particularly good and that can be used to improve its performance in relation to the critical success factors. A competency is *the ability to do something well*. Good facilities or a stable budget are not competencies in themselves; they are resources or *assets*, perhaps even *distinctive assets*, meaning they are hard for others to replicate; it is what you are able to do with these assets that might count as competencies. A *distinctive competency* is a competency that is difficult for others to replicate and so it is a source of enduring organizational advantage. A *core competency* is a competency central to the success of the organization. A *distinctive core competency* is not only central to the success of the organization but also helps the organization add more public value than alternative providers have. (*Examples* of distinctive core competencies might be ways of delivering services that are unique and especially valued by recipients, ways of maintaining the organization's reputation and people's trust in it that are far in excess of what rivals can do; see Bryson, 2011, Resource C; Eden & Ackermann, 2010).

Possible Desired Planning Outcomes

- Lists of internal strengths and weaknesses and external opportunities and challenges
- Identification of the organization's competencies and distinctive competencies—a special kind of strength—and especially those that are absolutely central to the success of the organization

- Key background reports
- Specific actions and ideas to build on strengths and take advantage of opportunities
- Specific actions and ideas to deal with challenges and weaknesses
- Thoughtful deliberations among key decision makers concerning strengths, weaknesses, opportunities, and challenges and their implications

Worksheet Directions

1. Consider using the snow card technique (see Resource C) with the strategic planning team (SPT) to develop an initial list of internal strengths and weaknesses and external opportunities and challenges. Fill out Worksheets 27 through 30.

2. If possible, always have the SPT consider what is going on outside the organization before it considers what is going on inside.

3. When the SPT is reviewing its SWOC/T list, encourage team members to look for patterns, important actions that might be taken immediately, and implications for the identification of strategic issues.

4. Consider using the organizational highs and lows exercise (Exercise 1) either as a prelude or follow-up to doing a SWOC analysis.

5. Take the time, if at all possible, to clearly identify the organization's competencies and especially its distinctive competencies (Worksheet 31), because they are crucial to effective pursuit of any strategy. If an organization doesn't have the ability (competency) to achieve a goal, that goal is just a New Year's resolution.

6. To ensure accuracy and reasonable completeness, conduct a follow-up analysis of the SWOC/T list developed by the SPT.

WORKSHEET 27

Internal Strengths

Instructions. Internal strengths are resources or capabilities that help an organization accomplish its mandates or mission.

1. Fill out as many worksheets as are necessary to derive a complete list. Put an asterisk (*) next to the eight to ten strengths you think are the most important. Discuss each of the high-priority strengths.

2. Identify any strategic issues that may be associated with the list.

3. Look at the list of options for preserving or enhancing strengths. Note with an asterisk (*) any that might be pursued immediately without unnecessarily or unwisely foreclosing future choices, then discuss.

Strength	Description	Options for Preserving or Enhancing Each Strength
Examples: • Highly skilled and motivated staff in Divisions A and B.	• All levels of staff in Divisions A and B are well trained and experienced. • Good morale in Divisions A and B.	• Maintain adequate compensation and reward levels. • Continue training programs. • Keep an effective perform-ance management system in place.
• Board is well-connected to most major external stakeholders.	• Good two-way communica-tions involving the board and most key external stakeholders.	• Work to find other ways to improve information and communications with remaining key stakeholders.

Strength	Description	Options for Preserving or Enhancing Each Strength

Worksheet 27

Internal Weaknesses

Instructions. Internal weaknesses are deficiencies in resources or capabilities that hinder an organization's ability to meet its mandates, fulfill its mission, and create public value. (*Examples:* poor internal and external communications, unclear mission or vision, structural misalignments, noncompetitive pay scales, low morale, inadequate resources.)

1. Fill out as many worksheets as are necessary to derive a complete list. Put an asterisk (*) next to the eight to ten weaknesses you think are the most important. Discuss each of the high-priority weaknesses.

2. Identify any strategic issues that may be associated with the list.

3. Look at the list of options for minimizing or overcoming the weaknesses. Note with an asterisk (*) any that might be pursued immediately without unnecessarily or unwisely foreclosing future choices, then discuss.

Weakness	Description	Options for Minimizing or Overcoming Weakness
Examples: • Lack of a clear, functional mission statement.	• We don't have a clear organizational mission.	• Review mandates and current mission statement. • Define a contemporary mission for the organization; involve appropriate stakeholders.

Weakness	Description	Options for Minimizing or Overcoming Weakness

Worksheet 28

Creating Your Strategic Plan, Third Edition.
Copyright © 2011 by John Wiley & Sons, Inc. All rights reserved.

WORKSHEET 29

External Opportunities

Instructions. External opportunities are primarily outside factors or situations that the organization can take advantage of to better fulfill its mission, meet its mandates, or create public value if any related challenges or threats can be mitigated. (*Examples:* new funding source, new potential service partner, chance to modify an outdated mandate, opportunity to pay off or refinance debt.)

1. Fill out as many worksheets as are necessary to derive a complete list. Put an asterisk (*) next to the eight to ten opportunities you think are the most important. Discuss each of the high-priority opportunities.

2. Identify any strategic issues that may be associated with the list.

3. Look at the list of options for taking advantage of the opportunities. Note with an asterisk (*) any that might be pursued immediately without unnecessarily or unwisely foreclosing future choices, then discuss.

Opportunity	Description	Options for Taking Advantage of Opportunity
Examples: • State has decided to change the way it funds social services.	• Develop a new revenue source by meeting a new or existing service need via the new funding mechanism.	• Evaluate mandates, mission, and existing services to identify impact of new funding mechanism on existing services. • Identify any service gaps that may be addressed or opened via the new funding arrangements. • Explore ways of responding to the funding changes that might preserve or add new revenue.

Opportunity	Description	Options for Taking Advantage of Opportunity

Worksheet 29

Creating Your Strategic Plan, Third Edition.
Copyright © 2011 by John Wiley & Sons, Inc. All rights reserved.

External Challenges (or Threats)

Instructions. External challenges are primarily outside factors or situations that can affect your organization in a negative way—making it harder to fulfill its mission, meet its mandates, or create public value. (*Examples:* loss of funding from an external source, new unfunded mandates, poor organizational image or reputation, poor union relations, lack of public support for key programs.)

1. Fill out as many worksheets as are necessary to derive a complete list. Put an asterisk (*) next to the eight to ten challenges you think are the most important. Discuss each of the high-priority challenges.

2. Identify any strategic issues that may be associated with the list.

3. Look at the list of options for overcoming the challenges. Note with an asterisk (*) any that might be pursued immediately without unnecessarily or unwisely foreclosing future choices, then discuss.

Challenge	Description	Options for Overcoming the Challenge
Examples: • Poor union relations. • Lack of public support.	• Developing a cooperative relationship between the organization's management and the union has been problematic. • Lack of public support for the organization and key programs.	• Work to involve the union in the strategic planning process. • Work to identify why the support is lacking. • Involve key stakeholders in the strategic planning process. • Build a communications outreach plan.

Challenge	Description	Options for Overcoming the Challenge

WORKSHEET 31

Competencies, Distinctive Competencies, and Distinctive Assets

Instructions. Use the following definitions in completing this worksheet.

Critical success factors (CSFs) are the things the organization must do, or criteria it must meet, in order for it to be successful in the eyes of its key stakeholders, especially those in its external environment.

Competencies are abilities, sets of actions, or strategies at which the organization is particularly good and that can be used to improve its performance in relation to the critical success factors. A competency is *the ability to do something well.* Good facilities or a stable budget are not competencies in themselves; they are resources. The things you are able to do with them might count as competencies.

A *distinctive competency* is a competency that is difficult for others to replicate and so it is a source of enduring organizational advantage.

A *core competency* is a competency central to the success of the organization.

A *distinctive core competency* is not only central to the success of the organization but also helps the organization add more public value than alternative providers have. (*Examples* of distinctive core competencies might be ways of delivering services that are unique and especially valued by recipients and ways of maintaining the organization's reputation and people's trust in it that are far in excess of what rivals can do.)

Distinctive assets are particular resources unique to the organization that may be drawn on or exploited by a competency. Competencies of all sorts require resources to run; if the resources in question are also distinctive, meaning not easily available to others, it will be easier to sustain those competencies over the long term.

A *core distinctive asset* is a distinctive asset that is central to the achievement of the organization's business aspirations.

1. Fill out the four columns on the next page. Use as many worksheets as you need.

2. Put an asterisk (*) next to competencies that are core competencies, then discuss.

3. Put a double asterisk (**) next to competencies that are distinctive core competencies, then discuss.

4. Discuss which assets are crucial to maintaining the competencies and distinctive competencies and also which assets count as distinctive assets (identify with a single asterisk [*]) and as core distinctive assets (identify with a double asterisk [**]).

Critical Success Factors	Reasons the Organization Does Well with the CSFs	Competencies—Capabilities the Organization Can Draw On to Do Well with the CSFs	Assets Drawn On or Exploited by the Competencies, or Necessary to Maintain the Competencies
Examples: • Services tailored to client needs	• Flexible scheduling system • Highly qualified staff	• Staff able to be flexible • Ability to make use of an excellent management information system that can match staff availability with client needs	• Excellent relationships with the union • Benefit package far better than competitors'—helps keep staff loyal and flexible • Excellent professional development program—helps staff stay on top of their field • Excellent relationship with local temporary staffing agency

Worksheet 31

Creating Your Strategic Plan, Third Edition. Copyright © 2011 by John Wiley & Sons, Inc. All rights reserved.

Critical Success Factors	Reasons the Organization Does Well with the CSFs	Competencies—Capabilities the Organization Can Draw On to Do Well with the CSFs	Assets Drawn On or Exploited by the Competencies, or Necessary to Maintain the Competencies

Worksheet 31

Creating Your Strategic Plan, Third Edition. Copyright © 2011 by John Wiley & Sons, Inc. All rights reserved.

Identify and Frame Strategic Issues

Purpose of Step

A *strategic issue* is a fundamental *policy choice* or *change challenge* affecting an organization's mandates, mission, product or service level and mix, clients or users, costs, financing, structure, processes, or management. The purpose of Step 5 is to identify the set of strategic issues facing the organization and to frame them as questions or concerns the organization can do something about.

The identification of strategic issues is the heart of the strategic planning process. The previous steps have been designed to provide several sources of information that will help you frame your organization's strategic issues in the most constructive way. The manner in which the issues are framed—and the clarity with which they are framed—will determine much of the subsequent politics of the process. Issue framing will also have a powerful impact on how goals and strategies are formulated, how stakeholders assess their interests and weigh the costs and benefits of alternative strategies, and whether specific arguments are likely to be winners or losers in support of various strategies.

Issue framing will also directly affect the ease with which the plan can be implemented. When participants support the way the issues are framed, they are far more likely to commit to the strategies developed in the next step and to subsequent strategy implementation.

Many important issues are likely to have emerged before this step in the process. They will have emerged from "planning to plan" meetings; stakeholder analyses; mission, values, and vision discussions; environmental scans; and SWOC/T discussions. And an important issue or issues may have prompted the strategic planning effort in the first place. You should have been capturing and documenting these potential strategic issues all along.

Issues fall into three main categories:

- Current issues that probably require immediate action

- Issues that are likely to require action in the near future but can be handled as part of the organization's regular planning cycle

- Issues that require no action at present but need to be continuously monitored

Over the course of the Strategy Change Cycle generally—and in this step specifically—a number of issues are likely to emerge that are more *operational*, or *tactical*, than *strategic*. It is important to capture the operational issues, for three reasons. First, many participants will think that these operational issues are the ones that have the most impact on their day-to-day work and will want to see something done about them. Second, finding ways to take action on these operational issues often energizes the strategic planning process—because people see that action as leading to immediate results that directly affect their work lives, and they gain confidence that the organization is serious about dealing with strategic concerns as well. And third, addressing operational issues often simultaneously removes barriers to effectively confronting the organization's strategic issues. (*Example of the difference between strategic and operational issues:* When an organization realizes it is experiencing ineffective use of information technology, resulting in inefficient work flows, poor communication, poor client record keeping, and unacceptably low levels of client service and satisfaction, it has identified a *strategic issue*. When that organization realizes it has a lack of office and off-site wireless telephone and Internet connectivity, it has identified a mostly *operational issue*.)

It is often helpful to create an operations team (OT) to explore the operational and tactical issues and develop recommendations for action. Having an OT will allow the strategic planning team (SPT) and strategic planning coordinating committee (SPCC) to stay focused on the strategic issues. As the SPT and SPCC identify operational and tactical issues—according to an agreed process and set of criteria—they will refer them to the OT for analysis, recommendations for action, and possible action. The OT might be a preexisting group of managers or else a small group composed of a cross-section of organizational employees.

Possible Desired Planning Outcomes

- An inclusive list of strategic and operational issues faced by the organization
- An ordering of the strategic issues in terms of priority, logic, sequence, or some other relevant classification
- Referral of operational issues to an operations team
- Creation of an OT if one does not already exist

Worksheet Directions

1. Have individual members of the strategic planning team fill out Worksheet 32, using one copy of the worksheet for each of five to nine possible issues identified.

2. Compare and contrast the individual responses given on Worksheet 32. Decide whether each issue is operational or strategic (or somewhere in between) by applying the information in Worksheet 33 after you have completed it. There is no absolute test to establish whether an issue is strategic or operational. Many issues will fall into a gray area, and the assessment of their strategic importance is a judgment that must be made by policymakers or top management. To assist leaders and managers in making this judgment, the questions in Worksheet 33 may be asked for each issue. Generally speaking, major strategic issues will be characterized by answers selected predominantly from columns 2 and 3 of Worksheet 33. Operational issues will tend to be characterized by answers selected predominantly from columns 1 and 2.

3. Have the team members work together to fill out Worksheet 34, the master list of key strategic issues. Work to ensure that the issues are clearly articulated.

4. Have the strategic planning team develop a master strategic issue statement for each issue, using Worksheet 35.

5. Decide on priorities among the issues on the master list (Worksheet 34). Consider using the dot technique for prioritizing. Start by placing the entire list of strategic issues on flipchart sheets. Then give each member of the strategic planning team five to seven colored stick-on dots, numbered in sequence from 1. He or she may "vote" for an issue by placing a dot next to it—*with the higher numbers reflecting higher priorities*. When everyone has thus indicated what he or she thinks are the most important strategic issues facing the organization, the weighted votes are tallied for each issue. The issues with the highest scores are strong candidates for becoming the key issues considered in the strategic planning process. Another approach is to develop a rating scale or criteria list to evaluate issues for their importance and criticality.

6. If necessary at this point, develop a new master list of key strategic issues (Worksheet 34).

7. If necessary at this point, develop new master strategic issue statements (Worksheet 35) for the key issues. Consider what your organization's goals might be in addressing each issue. Also remember that every strategic issue involves some form of conflict. Among the questions to be struggled over in the next step, strategy formulation, are the following:

- What will be done?

- How will it be done?

- Where will it be done?

- When will it be done; that is, what are the time frame and the timeline?

- Where will the resources come from to do it?
- Who will do it?
- Who will benefit by it—and who will not?
- Who must support it?

WORKSHEET 32

Individual Strategic Issue Identification

Instructions. This worksheet allows you as an individual to start to identify the set of strategic issues that the organization faces. A *strategic issue* is a fundamental *policy choice*, or *change challenge*, affecting an organization's mandates, mission, product or service level and mix, clients or users, costs, financing, organization, or management.

Complete a separate worksheet for each of the issues you identify; select five to nine issues.

_____

1. What is the issue? Be sure the issue is one the organization can do something about, and phrase the issue as a question that invites more than one answer. (*Example:* How best might our organization be structured, given that our current organizational structure does not allow us to effectively address our mandates or to fulfill our mission because it precludes development of team-based, interdisciplinary solutions to client problems?)

2. Why is this an issue? How is it related to the organization's SWOC/Ts, goals and objectives, ability to meet its mandates, fulfill its mission, and realize its vision? See the next two pages.

Strengths	Weaknesses	Opportunities	Challenges (or Threats)
Examples: • We have the staff we need to create team-based, interdisciplinary solutions that address client problems.	• Without an effective organizational structure, we are not able to serve the purposes for which we exist.	• A foundation grant can provide the planning and transition funding to support the move to a new organizational design.	• The support of key stakeholders is in jeopardy.

Strengths	Weaknesses	Opportunities	Challenges (or Threats)

Worksheet 32

Goals and Objectives	Mission	Mandates	Vision
Examples: • We have a goal of addressing client needs in a holistic, cost-effective way.	• We cannot fulfill our mission and are losing stakeholder support.	• We have mandates that we cannot meet.	• We envision clients who have become self-sustaining as a result of our integrated, cost-effective services.

Goals and Objectives	Mission	Mandates	Vision

Worksheet 32
Creating Your Strategic Plan, Third Edition.

3. What are the consequences of not addressing this issue? What makes it a priority? (*Example:* It is clear that a major challenge and issue is the need to address the organization's structure, which is a barrier to meeting its mandates and effectively fulfilling its mission.)

WORKSHEET 33

Operational Versus Strategic Issues

Instructions. There is no absolute test to establish whether an issue is strategic or operational. However, answering the questions in this worksheet will help policymakers or top management to make a judgment about this. Generally speaking, major strategic issues will be characterized by answers selected predominantly from columns 2 and 3 of this worksheet. Operational issues will tend to be characterized by answers selected predominantly from columns 1 and 2.

Issue:

The issue is:

❑ Primarily operational

❑ Both operational and strategic

❑ Primarily strategic

Operational ←——————————————→ Strategic

	Operational		Strategic
1. Would this issue, if put forward, make it onto the agenda of the organization's policy board (whether elected or appointed)?	No		Yes
2. Is the issue on (or should it be on) the agenda of the organization's chief executive (whether elected or appointed)?	No		Yes
3. When will the strategic issue's challenge or opportunity confront you?	Right now	Next year	Two or more years from now
4. How broad an impact will the issue have?	Single unit or division		Entire organization
5. How large is your organization's financial risk/opportunity?	Minor (10% of budget)	Moderate (10–15% of budget)	Major (25% of budget)

6. Will strategies for issue resolution likely require			
a. Changes in mandates or other rules governing the organization?	No		Yes
b. Changes in mission?	No		Yes
c. Changes in institutional or organizational design?	No		Yes
d. Development of new or elimination of existing service goals and programs?	No		Yes
e. Significant changes in revenue sources or amounts?	No		Yes
f. Major facility additions or modifications?	No		Yes
g. Significant staff expansion or retraction?	No		Yes
h. Important changes in stakeholder relations?	No		Yes
i. Major changes in technology?	No		Yes
j. Significant new learning?	No		Yes
k. Changes in the way strategy delivery is controlled in the present?	No		Yes
l. Development of significant future capabilities?	No		Yes
7. How apparent is the best approach for issue resolution?	Obvious, ready to implement	Broad parameters, few details	Wide open
8. What is the lowest level of management that can decide how to deal with this issue?	Line staff supervisor		Head of major department
9. What are the probable consequences of not addressing this issue?	Inconvenience, inefficiency	Significant service disruption, financial losses	Major long-term service disruption and large cost or revenue setbacks
10. How many other groups are affected by this issue and must be involved in resolution?	None	1–3	4 or more
11. How sensitive or "charged" is the issue relative to community, social, political, religious, and cultural values?	Benign	Touchy	Dynamite

Worksheet 33

Creating Your Strategic Plan, Third Edition.

WORKSHEET 34

Master List of Key Strategic Issues

Instructions.

1. Prepare a master list of key issues and each issue's likely sub-issues. They should be matters the organization can do something about and should be phrased as questions that have more than one answer.

2. After the list has been constructed, have team members discuss the order in which issues should be listed (for example, by overall importance, in logical order, or in the order in which they should be addressed).

3. Prepare a new version of the master list in which the issues and their sub-issues are presented in the preferred order.

Master List of Key Strategic Issues and Sub-Issues

1.

2.

3.

4.

5.

6.

7.

8.

9.

10.

11.

12.

13.

14.

15.

16.

WORKSHEET 35

Master Strategic Issue Statement

Instructions. The master list of key strategic issues (Worksheet 34) identifies the major policy questions or change challenges that are the focus of the strategic planning effort. Fill out a separate worksheet for each issue on this master list.

1. What is the issue? Be sure to phrase the issue as a question that has more than one answer. The issue should be one the organization can do something about.

2. Why is this an issue? Why does the issue exist? How is it related to the organization's mission, mandates, vision (if one exists), goals and objectives, internal strengths and weaknesses, and external opportunities and challenges (or threats)?

   • Mission

   • Mandates

   • Vision

   • Goals and objectives

- Strengths

- Weaknesses

- Opportunities

- Challenges (threats)

3. What are the consequences of not addressing this issue?

4. What should our (perhaps revised) goals be in addressing this issue?

Formulate Strategies to Manage the Issues

Purpose of Step

The purpose of Step 6 is to create a set of strategies to address each priority issue that has been identified in Step 5, so that the organization can better fulfill its mission, meet its mandates, achieve its issue-specific goals, and in general create public value.

Strategy is a *pattern* of purposes, policies, programs, projects, actions, decisions, and resource allocations that defines what an organization is, what it does, and why it does it. Strategies can vary by level, function, and time frame. Note as well that strategic planning can happen at all levels in an organization, meaning many strategic planning efforts will be intended for a part of the organization, not the organization as a whole.

Possible Desired Planning Outcomes

- Preparation of strategy statements of different kinds:

    Grand strategy statement for the organization as a whole

    Division or subunit strategy statements

    Program, service, product, project, or business process strategy statements

    Strategy statements for specific functions, such as human resource management, finance, and information technology

- Preparation of draft strategic plans

- Actions taken when they are identified and become useful or necessary

Worksheet Directions for Strategy Development

1. Remember that what is important is strategic thinking, acting, and learning, not a particular approach to strategy formulation or the development of a formal strategic plan. Step 6 is likely to be more interactive than previous steps because of the need to find the best fit among strategies and the elements of each strategy.

2. Develop answers to the questions on Worksheet 36 (Spencer, 1996), which may be filled out by boards, the strategic planning team (SPT), task forces, operational managers and selected staff, or others. The same people do not have to answer all of the questions.

   The strategic planning coordinating committee or the SPT may tackle the first five, for example, and other workgroups may be assigned the task of answering the next two. In some circumstances, answering the last two questions may be postponed until Step 7 (review and adopt the strategic plan) has been completed.

3. Have the SPT organize the Worksheet 36 responses into coherent sets of strategies, showing how the strategies address particular issues or achieve issue-specific or broader organizational goals and identifying the parts of the organization that will be required to implement the strategies. Prepare a strategy statement for each strategy, using a copy of Worksheet 37 for each one.

4. Make sure that strategies are described in reasonable detail, to allow people to make informed judgments about their efficacy and to provide reasonable guidance for assessing the implications for implementation and for the organization in general.

5. Ask the SPT to establish criteria for the evaluation of each suggested strategy. The team may use Worksheet 38, filling out one copy for each strategy.

6. Allow for consultation between the SPT and key stakeholders, so that the planning team can determine priorities among strategies for each issue or issue-related goal.

7. Develop a final strategy statement for each strategy, using the responses to Worksheets 36, 37, and 38 as a guide.

8. Encourage the SPT to develop a draft strategic plan. Information may be drawn from prior worksheets, and the checklist in Worksheet 39 may be used for deciding what should go in the plan.

Worksheet Directions for Plan Development

1. Prepare a draft strategic plan. Use the checklist in Worksheet 39 to decide what should go in the plan.

2. Even if you do not prepare a formal strategic plan, consider developing a set of interrelated strategy statements describing

   The grand strategy

   Organizational subunit strategies

Program, service, product, project, or business strategies

Functional strategies

3. Employ a structured process to review strategy statements and formal strategic plans. Review sessions may be structured around the following agenda:

Overview of plan

General discussion of plan and reactions to it

Brainstorming a list of the strengths and weaknesses of the plan (see Resource B for brainstorming guidelines)

Brainstorming a list of the opportunities and challenges (or threats) presented by the plan

Brainstorming a list of modifications to improve on strengths and take advantage of opportunities and minimize or overcome weaknesses and challenges (or threats)

Agreement on next steps to complete the plan

WORKSHEET 36

Some Key Questions for Identifying Strategies

Instructions. Fill out a separate worksheet for each key strategic issue. Be open to all ideas and build on the ideas of others. Challenge ideas (and the issue) in a constructive and positive way. Take the time to fully explore possible strategies. The idea is to develop lots of possible answers to each question before deciding what the best answers are through a deliberative process.

1. The strategic issue is:

   (*Example:* How can we make sure that in collaboration with our partners, clients receive the services they want and need and are satisfied with what we do to help them?)

2. Our issue-specific goals or desired outcomes are or should be (*or*, relevant broader organizational goals are or should be):

   (*Examples:* Significant improvements in client satisfaction, much better real-time feedback on organizational operations coupled with an ongoing organizational learning and performance improvement process, improved collaboration effectiveness with major partners.)

3. What are some practical alternatives, possibilities, or even visions we might pursue to address this issue and achieve our goal(s) or outcome(s)?

   (*Examples:* Establish appropriate and easy-to use client feedback mechanisms to gather performance-related data; create suitable forums for making use of performance data to improve performance; make better use of regular meetings, technology, newsletters, and other media to increase connections with collaboration partners as a step toward improving the collaboration's effectiveness.)

4. What are the possible barriers to our realizing these strategy alternatives?

   (*Examples:* Management resistance, poorly designed organizational structure, distance between offices, rigidities in organizational budgeting or financing.)

5. What major initiatives might we pursue to achieve these alternatives, dreams, or visions directly (or else indirectly through overcoming the barriers)?

   (*Examples:* Commission study of organizational client-oriented performance improvement processes; top management commits to making organizational learning a key part of performance improvement efforts; periodically survey collaboration partners to assess their views of the collaboration and how best it might improve.)

6. What are the key actions (with existing resources of people and dollars) that must be taken this year to implement the major initiatives? (Note that one kind of action within existing resources constraints is to figure out how major initiatives might be financed, including the possibility of reallocating existing funds to developing new resources to pay for the initiatives.)

   (*Examples:* Develop a request for proposals for the study of client-oriented performance improvement processes; develop an organizational learning structure and process proposal for review by key stakeholders; establish a monthly forum for collaboration partners and work with partners to assign responsibility for managing it.)

7. What specific steps could be taken within the next six months to implement the major initiatives, and who is responsible for taking them?

Step	Party Responsible
Examples:	
Develop a request for proposals for the study of client-oriented performance improvement processes.	Senior management team
Explore technology solutions to improve communications with collaboration partners.	IT director

Worksheet 36

WORKSHEET 37

Strategy Statement

Instructions. Prepare a separate strategy statement for each strategy. Describe strategies in enough detail that people can make informed judgments about their efficacy and start to assess the implications for implementation and for the organization in general.

1. What is the purpose of the strategy?

2. How might or should the strategy be named or designated?

3. What are the goals (or desired outcomes) of the strategy?

4. What are the principal components of the strategy, and how do they address the issue and achieve the issue-specific goals?

5. How will the strategy be financed?

6. What parts of the organization are required to implement the strategy?
    - ❑ Whole organization
    - ❑ Department(s)
    - ❑ Division(s)
    - ❑ Units
    - ❑ Function(s)

7. Which stakeholders and aspects of stakeholder relationships are crucial for effective implementation of the strategy?

Stakeholder	Crucial Aspects of Relationship

WORKSHEET 38

Criteria for Evaluating Suggested Strategies

Instructions. Identify the specific strategy to be evaluated and critique it against the criteria you have developed. Be sure to take the time to discuss and agree on the criteria to be used to evaluate the appropriateness of specific strategies. Do not overdo the number or strictness of the criteria; allow yourself and your team enough latitude to exercise judgment and make wise choices.

1. The issue the strategy is meant to address:

2. The proposed strategy:

3. Goals the strategy is meant to achieve:

4. Objectives:

5. Criteria to be used to evaluate this strategy:

Examples:

- Acceptability to and likely commitment from key decision makers, stakeholders, and opinion leaders
- Acceptability to the general public
- Client or user impact
- Relevance to addressing the issue at hand
- Consistency with or ability to change in needed ways:

  Vision

  Mission

  Mandates

  Values and philosophy

  Culture and belief systems

- Coordination or integration with other strategies, programs, and activities
- Technical feasibility
- Availability of or ability to acquire necessary technology
- Budget impacts, cost, and financing
- Assurance of necessary resource availability (money, staff, facilities, and so forth)
- Staff requirements in terms of needed competencies
- Incentives aligned in appropriate ways or ability to create needed alignments
- Cost effectiveness
- Return on investment
- Long-term impacts
- Short-term impacts
- Risk assessment
- Flexibility or adaptability
- Timing
- Facility requirements

Other appropriate criteria (insert your own criteria, especially strategy-specific criteria, here):

WORKSHEET 39

Checklist for Contents of the Strategic Plan

Instructions. Strategic plans vary in their content and design. Your organization may decide to use different plan formats for different purposes—for example, an executive summary for general distribution and a detailed plan for staff. The following checklist contains the typical elements that might be included in a plan (although not necessarily in the order shown here).

Audience for this version of the strategic plan: _____

Element	See Worksheet(s)	Include	
		Yes	No
❑ Executive summary			
❑ Introduction	8		
❑ Purpose	8		
❑ Process	8		
❑ Stakeholder participation	22, 23		
❑ Mission statement	24		
❑ Values statement	25		
❑ Vision statement	26, 42		
❑ Mandates	16, 17		
❑ Environmental analysis, including SWOC/Ts and competencies	27, 28, 29, 30, 31		
❑ Strategic issues	34, 35		
❑ Goals, objectives, performance indicators, and outcomes	19, 20, 24, 25, 35, 42, 45, 47		
❑ Grand strategy statement	36, 37, 38		
❑ Issue-specific strategies	34, 35, 36, 37, 38		
❑ Subunit strategy statements	36, 37, 38		
❑ Implementation and action plans	36, 37, 43, 44, 45, 47		
❑ Other related plans			
❑ Human resources	36, 37, 43, 44, 45, 47		
❑ Information technology	36, 37, 43, 44, 45, 47		
❑ Financial	36, 37, 43, 44, 45, 47		
❑ Communications	36, 37, 43, 44, 45, 47		
❑ Marketing	36, 37, 43, 44, 45, 47		
❑ Other	36, 37, 43, 44, 45, 47		
❑ Monitoring and evaluation plans	38, 49, 50		
❑ Plan for updating the plan	50, 51		

Review and Adopt the Strategic Plan

Purpose of Step

The purpose of Step 7 is to reach an official organizational decision to adopt and proceed with the strategic plan or plans. This step may merge with Step 6 (formulate strategies to manage the issues and prepare a draft strategic plan) in a single organization. But a separate step is likely to be necessary when strategic planning is undertaken for a large organization or for a collaboration or community. In the latter two cases the strategic planning coordinating committee (SPCC) will need to adopt the plan, and implementing organizations will also need to adopt it—or at least parts of it—in order for implementation to proceed effectively.

Step 7 generally marks the transition from strategic *planning* to ongoing strategic *management*.

Possible Desired Planning Outcomes

- Widely shared agreement on the strategic plan among key decision makers, and a decision to adopt the plan and proceed with implementation.

- Provision of the necessary guidance and resources for implementation. (It is important that the funding necessary to implement the plan be identified and allocated to the extent possible. Nothing is more disruptive to effective implementation and to the credibility of the planning effort than to have no resources for implementation.)

- Substantial support from internal and external stakeholders who can strongly affect implementation success.

- Widely shared sense of excitement about the substance and symbolism of the plan and the process.

Worksheet Directions

1. Determine who needs to be involved in reviewing and adopting the strategic plan (Worksheet 40).

   Continue to pay attention to the goals, concerns, and interests of all key stakeholders.

   Obtain necessary resource commitments, if at all possible, prior to the formal adoption session.

   Make sure that strategic planning and resultant recommendations or requests are linked to the budget cycle.

   Remember that material and nonmaterial incentives must reward behavior that will lead to effective implementation.

   Assess the nature and strength of supporting and opposing coalitions.

   Build support for the plan.

   Identify one or more sponsors and champions to help gain passage in the relevant arenas.

2. Have your team assess how best to reach key stakeholders.

   Reduce decision-maker uncertainty about the proposed plan.

   Develop arguments and counterarguments in support of the proposal prior to formal review sessions.

   Engage formal review bodies in structured review sessions that focus on proposal strengths, (perhaps) weaknesses, and modifications that would improve strategies (Worksheet 41).

   Remember that some people or groups may not want the plan to be adopted or implemented under any circumstances.

3. Appoint a lead person (writer) or a small team to produce the actual plan (if one has not already been prepared) and obtain the necessary reviews.

   Line up graphics, printing, and Web-focused communications support early in the process. Content is the substance of the plan; graphics provide the style. You need both in an appropriate design to make the plan an effective communications vehicle, and you need to make use of a variety of media—including Web-based media—to communicate about the plan. Great ideas badly presented can lose their greatness.

   Be prepared to bargain and negotiate over proposal features or other issues in exchange for support. This is part of the process.

   As part of ongoing communications efforts, provide public announcements of the plan's progress, at least within the organization and for key stakeholders and persons, groups, and organizations involved in the operational aspects of implementing strategies.

WORKSHEET 40

Plan Review and Adoption Process

Instructions. Have a small team from the organization conduct an initial review of the draft plan to catch any glaring problems. Consider using this group to lead the more formal review process, including communicating the contents of the draft plan and getting stakeholder feedback. Be inclusive in your plan review process.

1. Determine who needs to participate in reviewing and adopting the plan in order to achieve the maximum plan ownership. (Be inclusive.)

Plan Review	Plan Adoption

2. Review your stakeholder lists and assess who will likely support and who will likely oppose the plan or key plan elements; also assess what their "issue" is and why they have the stance they do.

Support	Opposition

3. Discuss what can be done to maintain plan support and to convert opposition to support.

4. Develop and communicate a plan review and adoption process.

What Will Be Done	Who Will Do It	When Will It Be Done	How Will It Be Done

5. Outline a communications and information process to inform stakeholders of the plan, the review process, and plan adoption. (*Examples:* meetings of all staff, memos, newsletters, meetings of particular groups, focus groups, Web-based presentations.)

6. To the extent possible, make sure *key* resources necessary for implementation are identified, and indicate whether or not they are assured. Do not forget personnel, information technology, and communications resources.

Resources	Assured		Included in Relevant Budgets or Staff Time Allocations	
	Yes	No	Yes	No

WORKSHEET 41

Plan Evaluation

Instructions. List the plan strengths and weaknesses and also modifications that would improve the plan. If time is short, skip the weaknesses and concentrate on strengths and modifications that would improve on the strengths.

This worksheet works best if it is first filled out by individuals, prior to a group discussion. As the group discussion proceeds, agreement may be reached on a shared list of plan strengths and weaknesses and also modifications that would improve the plan.

1. Strengths of the strategic plan:

2. Weaknesses of the strategic plan:

3. Modifications that would improve the strategic plan:

Establish an Effective Organizational Vision for the Future

Purpose of Step

In Step 8, an organizational *vision of success* is prepared, describing what the organization should look like as it successfully implements its strategies, fulfills its mission, meets its mandates, creates significant and lasting public value, and in general achieves its full potential. An organization typically has to go through more than one cycle of strategic planning before it can develop a truly effective vision for itself. A vision of success is therefore more likely to be a guide to strategy implementation than to strategy formulation.

All that is absolutely necessary to enhance organizational achievement is to identify a few key issues and do something effective about them. Nonetheless, if a vision of success can be prepared, it should be. Indeed a number of organizations will have prepared at least a sketch of a vision of organizational success in Step 3 and will then have used that sketch to guide subsequent steps in the process. A full-blown vision of success can be extremely important for educational purposes and for allowing people anywhere in the organization to take constructive action without constant oversight by leaders and managers.

Possible Desired Planning Outcomes

- Preparation of a short and inspiring vision of success
- Wide circulation of the vision among organizational members and other key stakeholders after appropriate consultations, reviews, and sign-offs
- Use of the vision to influence major and minor organizational decisions and actions

Worksheet Directions

1. Review the responses to Worksheet 26, if it has been used.

2. Have your team collect the available vision-related materials and documents. Review and discuss them; then consider developing a vision statement through individual work and group discussions with your team members and key stakeholders. Many of the elements of your organization's vision of success will have been described in the course of the strategic planning process. A vision of success should include the following information about the organization:

   Mission and the public value it creates

   Basic philosophy and core values

   Basic strategies

   Performance criteria

   Major decision rules

   Ethical standards applied to all employees

3. Have your team members or key stakeholder representatives break into small groups. First, each individual fills out Worksheet 42. Then the members of each small group share and discuss their answers, and finally the larger group discusses the results.

4. Following the discussion, request that someone prepare a draft vision statement. Circulate the draft to key stakeholders for their comments, and make modifications as appropriate until general agreement is reached. Communicate your organization's vision statement to key stakeholders, both internal and external.

5. Expect to revisit the vision statement throughout the implementation process and in the future. The vision will change as the organization and the factors affecting the organization change.

WORKSHEET 42

Vision of Success

Instructions. Fill out the worksheet first as an individual and then discuss with others.

1. What is the organization's mission? (See Worksheet 24.) Articulate the public value that the organization fulfills or should create. How will the world be better?

2. What are the organization's basic philosophies and core values? (See Worksheet 25.)

3. What are its basic strategies? (See Worksheet 37.)

4. What are the organization's performance criteria? (See Worksheets 16, 17, 19, 20, 24, 25, 34, 36, 37, and 38).

5. What are the major decision rules followed by the organization?

- What processes and procedures are followed to make major decisions?

- What is decided centrally?

- What is delegated?

- How are exceptions handled?

6. What are the ethical standards expected of all employees?

7. Draft a vision statement for your organization, based on your answers to the first six questions. An inspirational vision (see B. Shamir, M. Arthur, & R. House, "The Rhetoric of Charismatic Leadership: A Theoretical Extension, a Case Study, and Implications for Research," *The Leadership Quarterly,* 1994, *5*[1], 25–42; J. M. Kouzes & B. Z. Posner, *The Leadership Challenge*, 4th ed. [San Francisco: Jossey-Bass/Wiley, 2008]:

   • Focuses on a better future.

   • Encourages hopes, dreams, and noble ambitions.

   • Builds on (or reinterprets) the organization's history and culture to appeal to high ideals and common values.

   • Clarifies purpose and direction.

   • States positive outcomes.

   • Emphasizes the organization's uniqueness and distinctive competencies.

   • Emphasizes the strength of a unified group.

   • Uses word pictures, images, and metaphors.

   • Communicates enthusiasm, kindles excitement, and fosters commitment and dedication.

Develop an Effective Implementation Process

Purpose of Step

The purpose of Step 9 is to incorporate adopted strategies throughout the organization and its relevant organizational systems. The mere creation of a strategic plan is not enough. In the best of circumstances the plan will embody an agreement about what to do, how, where, when, why, and by whom, negotiated among and committed to by the members of the coalition necessary for guiding and protecting implementation efforts. But for the plan to be brought to life you also need an effective implementation process and set of action plans. It does not matter how outstanding the strategies and plan are if there is no capacity or will to carry them forward. (See the companion workbook, *Implementing and Sustaining Your Strategic Plan* [Bryson, Anderson, and Alston, 2011], for more extensive advice than can be provided here on how to plan and carry out an effective implementation process.)

It is worth repeating that implementation issues should be considered from the start of a strategic planning process. Implementation cannot be an afterthought if you want the strategic plan to be successfully implemented. During Step 6, on strategy development (see Worksheets 36 through 39), and Step 7, on plan review and adoption, a number of factors likely to dramatically affect implementation success should have been considered. For example:

- Having or building the necessary political will and external and internal support to make desirable changes

- Having the ability to commit the resources necessary to implement the plan in its entirety, or at least critical parts of it

- Being able to focus on what are agreed to be the highest priorities, or to have a strategy for making sure the highest priorities receive timely attention

- Finding ways to motivate key personnel to change, including aligning incentives appropriately

- Developing ways to change the organizational culture and belief system in desired directions

- Making necessary changes in organizational structures and processes

- Being able to make necessary changes in mandates

As implementation is planned and pursued, each of these items will become the focus for dialogue and deliberation. In other words, the dialogue and deliberation that are at the heart of strategic planning should continue throughout the implementation process, so that strategic thinking, acting, and learning are continuously fostered and the organization is helped to fulfill its mission, meet its mandates, realize its vision, and achieve its goals and objectives.

Furthermore, it also bears repeating that implementation does not need to wait until the strategic plan is done. Whenever wise implementing actions can be taken, they should be. Targeting "low-hanging fruit" and small wins for early action is a way of showing that things are going to change as a result of the time, effort, and resources expended on the planning process, and it will also build ongoing support for the process and make the more full-blown implementation effort easier.

Among all the challenges to effective implementation, a lack of resources is one of the most significant. Given the current economic stresses and national, state, and local resource constraints—the so-called new normal—public and nonprofit organizations alike are wrestling with how to support strategies and actions with necessary money, staff, facilities, equipment, and so forth. One of the most important lessons from experience is that not all actions require new money. Instead, the key to acquiring needed resources is often stopping doing something that is a lesser priority in order to fund something that is a higher priority. Many actions may be implemented just by shifting existing organizational resources around. Stopping doing one thing in order to do something that is more important may not be easy, but if an organization is unwilling or unable to shift resources to match its strategic priorities, then it probably should not have undertaken strategic planning in the first place.

Implementation Leadership

Implementation—like strategic planning generally—doesn't happen by itself. Leadership is absolutely essential. Leadership involves taking a proactive approach to implementation so that as strategies are implemented and actions taken, the next priorities in line have already been considered, can rise to the top, and be addressed. A proactive approach obviously includes deliberating with others about ways in which the factors affecting implementation success should be handled.

There are four key implementation leadership functions or roles; two are played by individuals and two by groups. These functions or roles are discussed further later in this step. They are the

- Implementation process sponsors (IPSs)

- Implementation process champions (IPCs)

- Implementation coordinating committee (ICC)

- Implementation recommendation and action teams (I-Teams)

Collectively, these roles or functions help to ensure adequate authority and power to legitimize, fund, and protect implementation efforts; managerial capacity to oversee day-to-day implementation activity; the ability to handle any cross-boundary coordination issues (that are essentially strategic and not just operational); and the teamwork necessary to do the heavy lifting around developing detailed, context-specific implementation recommendations and the taking of necessary implementation actions.

In smaller organizations, the strategic planning process sponsors and champions and the strategic planning coordinating committee (SPCC) and strategic planning team (SPT) may continue to oversee and guide the implementation process—in effect becoming the IPSs, IPCs, ICC, and I-Team. In larger organizations, however, new implementation process sponsors and champions, a new implementation coordinating committee (ICC), and new implementation recommendation and action teams (I-Teams) may be necessary. Usually there is some significant overlap between the old and new persons and groups to ensure adequate continuity and a more seamless move from planning to implementation. The operations team (OT) suggested in Step 5 is actually an I-Team charged with handling operational concerns, thus allowing the SPCC and SPT to continue to focus on strategic concerns by delegating operational matters to those who are charged with and can do something about them. However, it is very important that there be effective two-way communication and coordination between these groups (SPCC, SPT, and OT), so that they benefit from the exchange of ideas and understandings, which means that some overlap in membership across groups may be very helpful.

Implementation Process Sponsor

An implementation process sponsor (IPS) must have enough prestige, power, and authority to commit the organization to implementing the strategic plan and to hold people accountable for doing so. Implementation sponsors typically are top positional leaders—and often are the members of a policy board, cabinet, or executive committee acting collectively. They recognize or establish important features of the implementation context, make choices and commit resources that improve the chances for success, and pay careful attention to implementation progress along the way. They have a vested interest in achieving success and do what they can to make it happen. They also typically are important sources of knowledge about key issues and effective ways of addressing them and about the organization and its environment in general. They are likely to be especially knowledgeable about how to fit implementation efforts to key decision points.

The IPSs should have the following job description:

1. Articulate the purpose and importance of the implementation effort.

2. Commit necessary resources—time, money, energy, legitimacy—to the effort.

3. Emphasize throughout the implementation process that results are being and will be produced that are important to the organization's mission, mandates, and key stakeholders and that public value is being and will be created.

4. Encourage and reward hard work, smart and creative thinking, constructive dialogue, and multiple sources of input and insight aimed at ensuring successful implementation.

5. Be aware of the possible need for outside consultants.

6. Be willing to exercise power and authority to keep the process on track.

Implementation Process Champion

An implementation process champion (IPC) is a person appointed by the IPS to lead the implementation effort. IPCs have the primary responsibility for managing implementation efforts on a day-to-day basis. They are the ones who keep people on track, keep track of progress, and also pay attention to all the details. They model the kind of behavior they hope to get from other participants: reasoned, diligent, committed, enthusiastic, and good-spirited pursuit of the common good. They push, encourage, and coach implementers and other key participants through any difficulties. They need strong interpersonal skills, a commitment to getting the work done, and a good feel for how to manage complexity within the culture of the organization.

The IPCs should have the following job description:

1. Keep strategy and strategic plan implementation high on people's agendas.

2. Think about what has to come together (people, information, resources, completed work) at or before key decision points.

3. Keep rallying participants and pushing the implementation process along.

4. Develop process and agenda championship throughout the organization.

5. Be sensitive to power differences and able to engage all implementers and find ways to share power in order to increase the chances of implementation success.

Implementation Coordinating Committee

If the organization is large, many people need to be involved, and the situation is complex, then an implementation coordinating committee (ICC) or task force should probably be appointed. But keep in mind that there is a difference between giving people a seat on a committee and consulting with them as part of the process. The gains from involving people may not require actually appointing these individuals to the ICC. Unless membership in the committee is limited, it may become too large to be effective. If an organization is the focus of attention, the ICC will typically include a cross-section of organizational members by level and function and perhaps representatives of key external stakeholder groups as well. That said, the group probably should number no more than nine members. If necessary, there may be a large representative and legitimizing body, and a small executive committee that engages in the most extensive discussions and makes recommendations to the larger group. For a collaboration or community, a large, representative legitimizing body could coordinate the process and smaller representative bodies could attend to specific issue areas.

The ICC should have a charter that includes at least the following responsibilities:

1. Serve as a forum for deliberation, consultation, negotiation, problem solving, or buffering among organizations, units, groups, or persons involved.

2. Ensure that all members allocate the quality time necessary to help the ICC do its job effectively.

3. Record all decisions or recommendations in writing and circulate them to key stakeholder groups.

4. Where appropriate, approve recommendations and decisions made by the I-Team(s), or serve as an advisory body to formal decision makers or policy-making bodies regarding implementation issues.

5. Rotate membership of the group if it is to be a standing committee overseeing annual and multiyear implementation efforts, in order to keep new ideas flowing and widen involvement in the process.

Implementation Recommendation and Action Team

The implementation recommendation and action team (I-Team) develops recommendations on strategic plan implementation in order to facilitate, connect, and coordinate structures, processes, resources, or activities across organizational boundaries in ways required for successful implementation. I-Teams may also be authorized to take implementing actions not requiring high-level approval. The I-Team members are selected by the IPS and IPC, often in consultation with the ICC—although it is also advisable to seek advice from the rest of the organization and selected external stakeholders, as our experience shows that such broadly based advice is very helpful in getting buy-in and support for the implementation process.

An I-Team should be able to do the following and perhaps have these responsibilities stated in a formal charter:

1. Focus collective attention, across all types of boundaries, on strategy and strategic plan implementation tasks, responsibilities, progress, and needed further action.

2. Make recommendations to the organization's leadership on implementation steps and actions.

3. Help with coordinating the implementation process and tasks across boundaries.

4. Take action within authorized limits.

5. Help to rally key participants and push the implementation process along.

6. Provide a venue in which power is shared.

7. Offer a setting where important conflicts may be explored and managed effectively.

8. Provide occasions for the development of implementation championship throughout the organization.

Implementation leaders and groups should keep asking themselves:

• What is the best thing to do at this time, and what is necessary to accomplish it?

• Is what we are trying to do achievable?

   Is the objective realistic?

   Are there adequate resources? If not, how can we get them?

• Why is the objective significant for meeting our mandates, fulfilling our mission, realizing our vision, and creating public value?

• How do (or should) implementing actions in one area affect ongoing or new strategy implementation in other areas?

• How will we know when we have achieved our goals and objectives?

• When will the objective be accomplished, and by whom?

Specific project management tools may be particularly useful as implementation resources. For example, there are many project management software programs available, with varying levels of functionality and cost (such as BaseCamp or Microsoft Project).

Possible Desired Implementation Outcomes

- Added public value through goal achievement and heightened stakeholder satisfaction

- Clear understanding of what needs to be done, by whom, when, where, how, and why

- Reasonably smooth and rapid introduction of the strategies throughout the relevant systems; adoption of the changes by all relevant organizations, units, groups, and individuals in a timely fashion

- Development of a widely shared vision of success that guides implementation (if this vision has not been developed earlier)

- Use of a *debugging* process to identify and fix the difficulties that almost inevitably arise as a new strategy is put into place

- Assurance that important features of the strategies are maintained throughout the implementation process

    Use of a formal evaluation process to determine whether substantive and symbolic strategic goals have been achieved

    Establishment of or provision for review points, at which maintenance, replacement, or termination of the strategies can be considered

- Timely updating of the strategic plan and relevant implementation plans

- Capacity built for the next round of strategic planning

Worksheet Directions

1. Think strategically about implementation (as we hope you have from the start of the strategic planning process). Consciously manage implementation so that important public and nonprofit purposes are furthered and public value is created.

2. Clearly document your organization's existing strategy, program, product, service, and project priorities, using Worksheet 43. An understanding of what the organization is currently doing is the starting point for the effective integration of strategic planning priorities. The organization will need to shift some (or in rare circumstances all) of its efforts and resources to the higher-level priorities reflected in the strategic plan in order to ensure effective implementation.

3. Using Worksheet 44, assess the new strategic plan's strategy, program, product, service, and project impacts. (Use this worksheet to assess any new strategies that emerge during implementation as well.)

4. Then use Worksheet 45 to reconcile the organization's current activities with those envisioned in the strategic plan.

5. Consider developing one or more I-Teams for carrying out the reconciled list of priorities from Worksheet 45. Use Worksheet 46 to help create each I-Team. The membership of the I-Team may be the same as that of the SPT, especially in small organizations, but in large or complex organizations it is likely to be different from the SPT's, although some overlap in membership is typically desirable.

6. For each strategy developed through the strategic planning process, develop a clearly defined implementation and action plan (Worksheet 47) that answers the who, what, how, where, and when questions. The responsibility for creating each action plan may be given to the I-Team(s). Whether there is an I-Team or not, involve the operational and administrative stakeholders in this key step. The organization's resource situation and mandates may make a phased approach to the implementation of the strategic plan necessary. Action plans, which must be carefully coordinated, should detail

   Specific expected results, objectives, and milestones

   Roles and responsibilities of implementation bodies, teams, and individuals

   Specific action steps

   Schedules

   Resource requirements and sources

   A communication process

   A review, monitoring, and readjustment process

   Accountability processes and procedures

7. Consider organizing and keeping track of the implementation process by using project management software. Worksheet 48 is a blank Microsoft Project worksheet. Exhibit 2, following Worksheet 48, presents a Microsoft Project screenshot of the action plan of an actual strategy implementation project that shows a set of strategies and their associated actions with timelines and responsibilities identified. Other project management software products also work well; for example, BaseCamp.

8. Use the Strategy/Action Status Report Form (Worksheet 49) to keep all initiatives on track, using a separate form for each initiative and action.

Evaluating Priorities for Existing Strategies, Programs, Products, Services, and Projects

Existing Strategies, Programs, Products, Services, Projects	Criteria for Establishing Priority, Including (at Least) Impact on Mandates, Mission, Key Stakeholders, and Organization; Ability to Deliver Desired Outcomes	Priority (low, moderate, or high)	Resources Used			Time Frame
			People	Financial	Other Resources	

WORKSHEET 44

Evaluating Priorities for Proposed New Strategies, Programs, Products, Services, and Projects

Proposed New Strategies, Programs, Products, Services, Projects	Criteria for Establishing Priority, Including (at Least) Impact on Mandates, Mission, Key Stakeholders, and Organization; Ability to Deliver Desired Outcomes	Priority (low, moderate, high)	Resources Needed			Time Frame
			People	Financial	Other Resources	

WORKSHEET 45

Prioritizing Strategies, Programs, Products, Services, and Projects

Instructions. Using Worksheets 43 and 44, compile a master list of priorities that reconciles the organization's current strategies, programs, products, services, and projects with those proposed in the strategic plan.

Existing Priorities That Should Be Retained (strategies, programs, products, services, projects)	Strategic Plan Priorities That Should Be Pursued (strategies, programs, products, services, projects)

WORKSHEET 46

Creating Implementation Recommendation and Action Teams (I-Teams)

Instructions. This worksheet is designed to assist the implementation process sponsors and champions (and perhaps the ICC) decide who should be on the implementation recommendation and action team(s) (I-Team). In small organizations making these choices will be relatively easy, but in large or complex organizations making suitable choices will take time, consultation with others, and careful consideration.

The first step in determining I-Team members is to make sure the IPS and IPC have a clear picture (often an actual graphic picture) of the organization, its structure, the key functions it performs, and its major personnel classifications (see Step 8). The second step is to gain clarity about what the implementation agenda is, including exactly what strategies are to be implemented and what major actions are to be taken. The IPS and IPC should use Worksheet 26 and also Worksheets 34, 35, 36, 37, and 38 to help achieve necessary clarity. This information will then guide the determination of who needs to be involved in the implementation process in order to ensure successful implementation of agreed strategies and actions. Implementation in organizations is greatly dependent on buy-in from employees at all levels and often other key stakeholders, so getting the right people on the I-Team is often vital to achieving success.

The IPS and IPC, along with perhaps the ICC and other key internal and external stakeholders, should then be asked: What are the most important things we are trying to achieve through the implementation process? What are the major strategies and bundles of related actions we are trying to implement? For each strategy an initial starting list of key actions should be created. List what is proposed to be done, when it should be done, who needs to be involved, what resources are needed, and how the action initiatives will be overseen and managed.

Strategy to be implemented: _____

1. What exactly is to be implemented? List major elements and accompanying actions to be taken to implement the strategy.

    •

    •

-

-

-

-

Comments:

2. In order for the strategy to be successfully implemented, which organizational units or groups both across and down in the organization need to be involved?

   -

   -

Creating Your Strategic Plan, Third Edition.
Copyright © 2011 by John Wiley & Sons, Inc. All rights reserved.

-

-

-

Comments:

3. What major organizational functions (for example, service delivery, finance, communications, human resources, information technology, administration, and so on) should be represented in this effort?

-

-

-

-

-

Comments:

4. Specifically *who* should be considered for membership on the I-Team?

-

-

-

-

-

-

-

-

-

-

-

-

-

Comments:

5. Does the previous list ensure that all major necessary job classifications (from management to supervisory to line workers) are represented?

    ❑ Yes

    ❑ No

    If no, which classifications are missing? Who might be considered who fits these classifications?

    •

    •

    •

    •

    •

    Comments:

6. Is representation from external stakeholders—for example, outside boards, unions, funders, clients, and so on—necessary?

❑ Yes

❑ No

If yes, which stakeholders should be involved?

•

•

•

•

•

Comments:

7. Are all internal and external stakeholders with or likely to have major concerns represented?

❏ Yes

❏ No

If no, who is missing?

-

-

-

-

-

Comments:

8. Who should be involved to ensure that we have the organization's key functional knowledge areas, skills, and competencies represented? Who should be included who knows the organization's history and how to get things done? Who should be included who is a good communicator or is a key opinion leader or is politically well connected or is trusted by many or does really good work?

   •

   •

   •

   •

   •

   Comments:

9. Keep adding names to the list. The results are to be kept confidential and are to be used by the organization's leadership, the IPS, the IPC, and the ICC to inform selection of the I-Team.

10. In the final analysis, who should be on the I-Team?

    •

    •

    •

    •

    •

    •

    •

    •

    •

    •

WORKSHEET 47

Action Planning

Instructions. For each priority listed on Worksheet 45, explore the following aspects of an action plan.

1. Priority strategy:

2. What goal or goals are to be achieved via this strategy?

3. What specific actions must be taken to implement the strategy in the next six months to a year? What will be done, when, and where?

4. What are the expected outcomes, results, and milestones? Which stakeholders will benefit and how?

5. Who will lead the effort and who will do what to implement the actions? What are these individuals' or groups' roles and responsibilities?

6. What resources will be required, and where will they be obtained?

   a. Funds

   b. People

   c. Technology

   d. Other

7. How will the action plan be communicated to stakeholders?

8. How will implementation of the action plan be reviewed and monitored and accountability ensured?

WORKSHEET 48

Microsoft Project Schedule Template

ID	Task Name	Duration	Start	Finish	Predecessors	Resource Names	Qtr 4, 2011 Oct	Nov	Dec	Qtr 1, 2012 Jan	Feb	Mar	Qtr 2, 2012 Apr	May	Jun
1															
2															
3															
4															
5															
6															
7															
8															
9															
10															
11															
12															
13															
14															
15															
16															
17															
18															

Project: Sample MS Project Template
Date: Tue 07-27-11

Task	Milestone ◆	External Tasks
Split	Summary	External Milestone ◆
Progress	Project Summary	Deadline ⇩

Page 1

ID	Task Name	Duration	Start	Finish	Predecessors	Resource Names	Qtr 4, 2011			Qtr 1, 2012			Qtr 2, 2012		
							Oct	Nov	Dec	Jan	Feb	Mar	Apr	May	Jun
19															
20															
21															
22															
23															
24															
25															
26															
27															
28															
29															
30															

Project: Sample MS Project Template
Date: Tue 07-27-11

Task		Milestone	◆
Split		Summary	
Progress		Project Summary	

External Tasks	
External Milestone	◆
Deadline	⇩

Page 2

Worksheet 48

Creating Your Strategic Plan, Third Edition. Copyright © 2011 by John Wiley & Sons, Inc. All rights reserved.

EXHIBIT 2
Microsoft Project Schedule Template

Los Angeles County—Comprehensive Educational Reform in the Juvenile Halls and Camps

ID	Task Name	Start	Finish
1	**Educational Responsibilities**	**Wed 03-04-09**	**Fri 12-31-10**
2	**1. Recruit Director of School Services**	**Wed 03-04-09**	**Wed 06-30-10**
3	a. Conduct 1st round of recruitment	Wed 03-04-09	Fri 09-04-09
4	b. Conduct 2nd round of recruitment	Mon 10-05-09	Fri 03-26-10
5	c. Hire Director of School Services	Mon 03-29-10	Mon 03-29-10
6	d. Orient & coach Director of School Services	Mon 03-29-10	Wed 06-30-10
7	**2. Implement assessment MDTs**	**Mon 07-27-09**	**Fri 03-26-10**
8	a. Pilot camp assessment/case planning	Mon 07-27-09	Fri 10-02-09
9	b. Obtain approval of juvenile bureaus	Mon 10-05-09	Fri 10-16-09
10	c. Present to JC delinquency judges	Tue 10-20-09	Tue 10-20-09
11	d. Complete flowscript/other documentation	Tue 10-20-09	Fri 10-30-09
12	e. Complete training of CAU/CHQ staff	Tue 10-20-09	Fri 10-30-09
13	f. Update County FERPA MOU to support MDTs	Mon 11-02-09	Fri 12-25-09
14	g. Upcate County HIPPA MOU to support MDTs	Mon 11-02-09	Fri 12-25-09
15	h. Obtain approvals of FERPA/HIPPA MOUs	Mon 01-04-10	Fri 03-26-10
16	**3. Ensure parent role in youth development**	**Mon 06-15-09**	**Fri 12-31-10**
17	a. Produce initial module of parent training	Mon 06-15-09	Fri 09-11-09
18	b. "Field test" initial module of parent training	Mon 09-14-09	Fri 10-09-09
19	c. Prioritize production of remaining modules	Mon 09-14-09	Fri 10-09-09
20	d. Roll out initial module of parent training	Mon 11-02-09	Fri 12-25-09
21	e. Produce Phase II parent training modules	Mon 01-04-10	Wed 06-30-10
22	f. Produce Phase III parent training modules	Thu 07-01-10	Fri 12-31-10
23	**4. Work with judges to determine ed. rights**	**Mon 04-06-09**	**Fri 01-29-10**
24	a. Recruit Junior Women's volunteers	Mon 04-06-09	Fri 06-26-09
25	b. Train Junior Women's volunteers	Mon 06-29-09	Fri 07-31-09
26	c. Review use of Junior Women's volunteers	Mon 01-04-10	Fri 01-29-10
27	**5. Work with judges to ID surrogates**	**Mon 11-02-09**	**Fri 05-28-10**
28	a. Recruit surrogates	Mon 11-02-09	Fri 12-25-09
29	b. Train surrogates	Mon 01-04-10	Fri 02-26-10
30	c. Review use of surrogates	Mon 04-05-10	Fri 05-28-10
31	**6. Train DPOs to advocate for youth**	**Tue 11-03-09**	**Fri 10-01-10**
32	a. Develop training materials	Tue 11-03-09	Thu 12-31-09
33	b. Obtain STC certification	Mon 01-04-10	Fri 01-29-10
34	c. Train camp DPOs	Mon 02-01-10	Wed 06-30-10
35	d. Train juvenile field DPOs	Mon 02-01-10	Wed 06-30-10
36	e. Conduct fidelity assessment of staff	Mon 07-05-10	Fri 10-01-10

Project: Compreh. Education Reform
Date: Sat 10-03-09

Task Requiring Resources
Progress
Ongoing Task
Completed Task
Milestone ◆
Summary

Page 1

EXHIBIT 2

Microsoft Project Schedule Template (*Continued*)

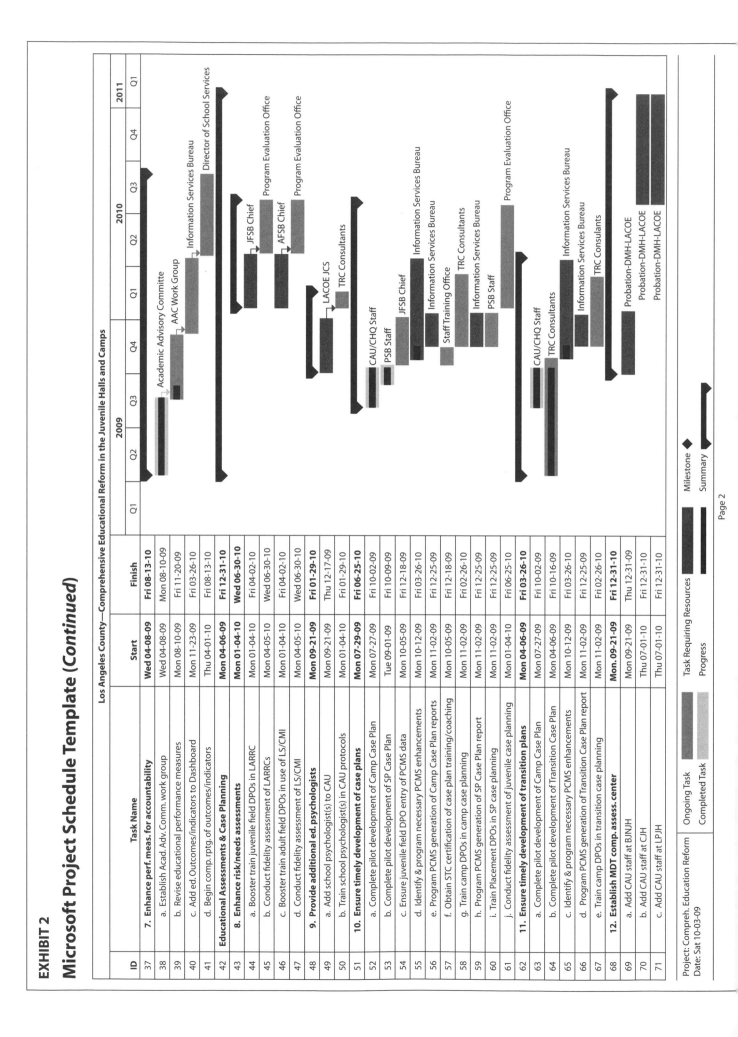

Los Angeles County—Comprehensive Educational Reform in the Juvenile Halls and Camps

ID	Task Name	Start	Finish
37	**7. Enhance perf. meas. for accountability**	**Wed 04-08-09**	**Fri 08-13-10**
38	a. Establish Acad. Adv. Comm. work group	Wed 04-08-09	Mon 08-10-09
39	b. Revise educational performance measures	Mon 08-10-09	Fri 11-20-09
40	c. Add ed. Outcomes/indicators to Dashboard	Mon 11-23-09	Fri 03-26-10
41	d. Begin comp. rptg. of outcomes/indicators	Thu 04-01-10	Fri 08-13-10
42	**Educational Assessments & Case Planning**	**Mon 04-06-09**	**Fri 12-31-10**
43	**8. Enhance risk/needs assessments**	**Mon 01-04-10**	**Wed 06-30-10**
44	a. Booster train juvenile field DPOs in LARRC	Mon 01-04-10	Fri 04-02-10
45	b. Conduct fidelity assessment of LARRCs	Mon 04-05-10	Wed 06-30-10
46	c. Booster train adult field DPOs in use of LS/CMI	Mon 01-04-10	Fri 04-02-10
47	d. Conduct fidelity assessment of LS/CMI	Mon 04-05-10	Wed 06-30-10
48	**9. Provide additional ed. psychologists**	**Mon 09-21-09**	**Fri 01-29-10**
49	a. Add school psychologist(s) to CAU	Mon 09-21-09	Thu 12-17-09
50	b. Train school psychologist(s) in CAU protocols	Mon 01-04-10	Fri 01-29-10
51	**10. Ensure timely development of case plans**	**Mon 07-29-09**	**Fri 06-25-10**
52	a. Complete pilot development of Camp Case Plan	Mon 07-27-09	Fri 10-02-09
53	b. Complete pilot development of SP Case Plan	Tue 09-01-09	Fri 10-09-09
54	c. Ensure juvenile field DPO entry of PCMS data	Mon 10-05-09	Fri 12-18-09
55	d. Identify & program necessary PCMS enhancements	Mon 10-12-09	Fri 03-26-10
56	e. Program PCMS generation of Camp Case Plan reports	Mon 11-02-09	Fri 12-25-09
57	f. Obtain STC certification of case plan training/coaching	Mon 10-05-09	Fri 12-18-09
58	g. Train camp DPOs in camp case planning	Mon 11-02-09	Fri 02-26-10
59	h. Program PCMS generation of SP Case Plan report	Mon 11-02-09	Fri 12-25-09
60	i. Train Placement DPOs in SP case planning	Mon 11-02-09	Fri 12-25-09
61	j. Conduct fidelity assessment of juvenile case planning	Mon 01-04-10	Fri 06-25-10
62	**11. Ensure timely development of transition plans**	**Mon 04-06-09**	**Fri 03-26-10**
63	a. Complete pilot development of Camp Case Plan	Mon 07-27-09	Fri 10-02-09
64	b. Complete pilot development of Transition Case Plan	Mon 04-06-09	Fri 10-16-09
65	c. Identify & program necessary PCMS enhancements	Mon 10-12-09	Fri 03-26-10
66	d. Program PCMS generation of Transition Case Plan report	Mon 11-02-09	Fri 12-25-09
67	e. Train camp DPOs in transition case planning	Mon 11-02-09	Fri 02-26-10
68	**12. Establish MDT comp. assess. center**	**Mon. 09-21-09**	**Fri 12-31-10**
69	a. Add CAU staff at BJNJH	Mon 09-21-09	Thu 12-31-09
70	b. Add CAU staff at CJH	Thu 07-01-10	Fri 12-31-10
71	c. Add CAU staff at LPJH	Thu 07-01-10	Fri 12-31-10

Project: Compreh. Education Reform
Date: Sat 10-03-09

Task Requiring Resources

Progress

Ongoing Task

Completed Task

Milestone

Summary

Page 2

Los Angeles County—Comprehensive Educational Reform in the Juvenile Halls and Camps

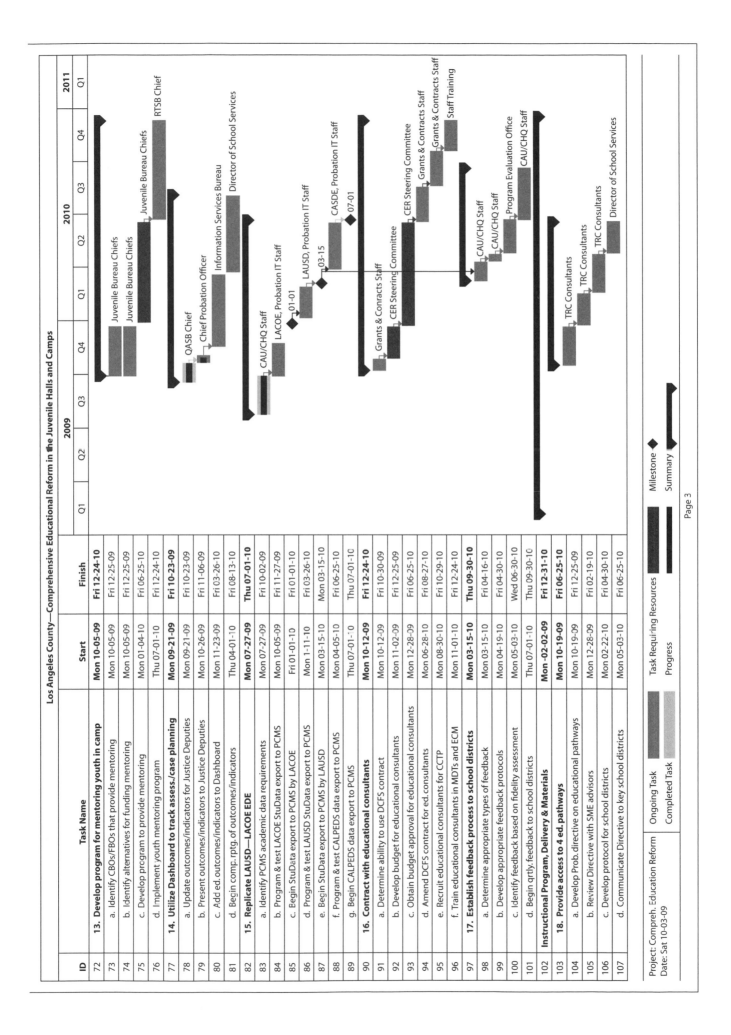

ID	Task Name	Start	Finish
72	**13. Develop program for mentoring youth in camp**	**Mon 10-05-09**	**Fri 12-24-10**
73	a. Identify CBOs/FBOs that provide mentoring	Mon 10-05-09	Fri 12-25-09
74	b. Identify alternatives for funding mentoring	Mon 10-05-09	Fri 12-25-09
75	c. Develop program to provide mentoring	Mon 01-04-10	Fri 06-25-10
76	d. Implement youth mentoring program	Thu 07-01-10	Fri 12-24-10
77	**14. Utilize Dashboard to track assess./case planning**	**Mon 09-21-09**	**Fri 10-23-09**
78	a. Update outcomes/indicators for Justice Deputies	Mon 09-21-09	Fri 10-23-09
79	b. Present outcomes/indicators to Justice Deputies	Mon 10-26-09	Fri 11-06-09
80	c. Add ed. outcomes/indicators to Dashboard	Mon 11-23-09	Fri 03-26-10
81	d. Begin comp. rptg. of outcomes/indicators	Thu 04-01-10	Fri 08-13-10
82	**15. Replicate LAUSD—LACOE EDE**	**Mon 07-27-09**	**Thu 07-01-10**
83	a. Identify PCMS academic data requirements	Mon 07-27-09	Fri 10-02-09
84	b. Program & test LACOE StuData export to PCMS	Mon 10-05-09	Fri 11-27-09
85	c. Begin StuData export to PCMS by LACOE	Fri 01-01-10	Fri 01-01-10
86	d. Program & test LAUSD StuData export to PCMS	Mon 1-11-10	Fri 03-26-10
87	e. Begin StuData export to PCMS by LAUSD	Mon 03-15-10	Mon 03-15-10
88	f. Program & test CALPEDS data export to PCMS	Mon 04-05-10	Fri 06-25-10
89	g. Begin CALPEDS data export to PCMS	Thu 07-01-10	Thu 07-01-10
90	**16. Contract with educational consultants**	**Mon 10-12-09**	**Fri 12-24-10**
91	a. Determine ability to use DCFS contract	Mon 10-12-09	Fri 10-30-09
92	b. Develop budget for educational consultants	Mon 11-02-09	Fri 12-25-09
93	c. Obtain budget approval for educational consultants	Mon 12-28-09	Fri 06-25-10
94	d. Amend DCFS contract for ed. consultants	Mon 06-28-10	Fri 08-27-10
95	e. Recruit educational consultants for CCTP	Mon 08-30-10	Fri 10-29-10
96	f. Train educational consultants in MDTs and ECM	Mon 11-01-10	Fri 12-24-10
97	**17. Establish feedback process to school districts**	**Mon 03-15-10**	**Thu 09-30-10**
98	a. Determine appropriate types of feedback	Mon 03-15-10	Fri 04-16-10
99	b. Develop appropriate feedback protocols	Mon 04-19-10	Fri 04-30-10
100	c. Identify feedback based on fidelity assessment	Mon 05-03-10	Wed 06-30-10
101	d. Begin qrtly. feedback to school districts	Thu 07-01-10	Thu 09-30-10
102	**Instructional Program, Delivery & Materials**	**Mon -02-02-09**	**Fri 12-31-10**
103	**18. Provide access to 4 ed. pathways**	**Mon 10-19-09**	**Fri 06-25-10**
104	a. Develop Prob. directive on educational pathways	Mon 10-19-09	Fri 12-25-09
105	b. Review Directive with SME advisors	Mon 12-28-09	Fri 02-19-10
106	c. Develop protocol for school districts	Mon 02-22-10	Fri 04-30-10
107	d. Communicate Directive to key school districts	Mon 05-03-10	Fri 06-25-10

Milestone ◆ Summary

Task Requiring Resources
Progress

Ongoing Task
Completed Task

Project: Compreh. Education Reform
Date: Sat 10-03-09

Page 3

EXHIBIT 2

Microsoft Project Schedule Template (*Continued*)

Los Angeles County—Comprehensive Educational Reform in the Juvenile Halls and Camps

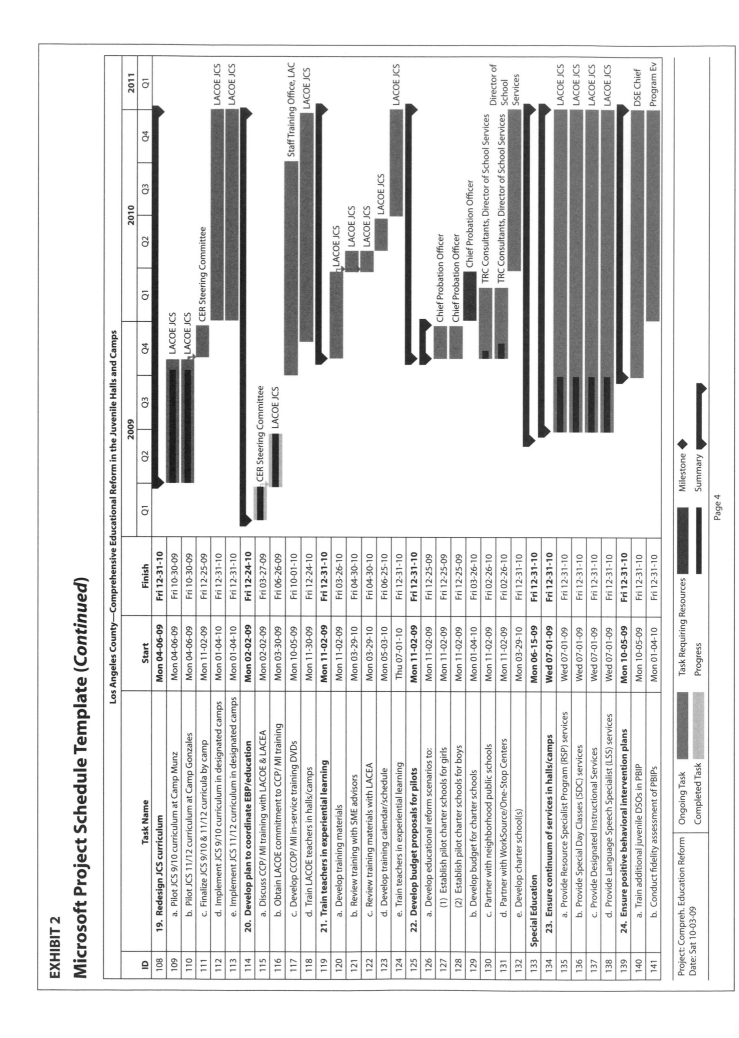

ID	Task Name	Start	Finish
108	**19. Redesign JCS curriculum**	**Mon 04-06-09**	**Fri 12-31-10**
109	a. Pilot JCS 9/10 curriculum at Camp Munz	Mon 04-06-09	Fri 10-30-09
110	b. Pilot JCS 11/12 curriculum at Camp Gonzales	Mon 04-06-09	Fri 10-30-09
111	c. Finalize JCS 9/10 & 11/12 curricula by camp	Mon 11-02-09	Fri 12-25-09
112	d. Implement JCS 9/10 curriculum in designated camps	Mon 01-04-10	Fri 12-31-10
113	e. Implement JCS 11/12 curriculum in designated camps	Mon 01-04-10	Fri 12-31-10
114	**20. Develop plan to coordinate EBP/education**	**Mon 02-02-09**	**Fri 12-24-10**
115	a. Discuss CCP/ MI training with LACOE & LACEA	Mon 02-02-09	Fri 03-27-09
116	b. Obtain LACOE commitment to CCP/ MI training	Mon 03-30-09	Fri 06-26-09
117	c. Develop CCOP/ MI in-service training DVDs	Mon 10-05-09	Fri 10-01-10
118	d. Train LACOE teachers in halls/camps	Mon 11-30-09	Fri 12-24-10
119	**21. Train teachers in experiential learning**	**Mon 11-02-09**	**Fri 12-31-10**
120	a. Develop training materials	Mon 11-02-09	Fri 03-26-10
121	b. Review training with SME advisors	Mon 03-29-10	Fri 04-30-10
122	c. Review training materials with LACEA	Mon 03-29-10	Fri 04-30-10
123	d. Develop training calendar/schedule	Mon 05-03-10	Fri 06-25-10
124	e. Train teachers in experiential learning	Thu 07-01-10	Fri 12-31-10
125	**22. Develop budget proposals for pilots**	**Mon 11-02-09**	**Fri 12-31-10**
126	a. Develop educational reform scenarios to:	Mon 11-02-09	Fri 12-25-09
127	(1) Establish pilot charter schools for girls	Mon 11-02-09	Fri 12-25-09
128	(2) Establish pilot charter schools for boys	Mon 11-02-09	Fri 12-25-09
129	b. Develop budget for charter schools	Mon 01-04-10	Fri 03-26-10
130	c. Partner with neighborhood public schools	Mon 11-02-09	Fri 02-26-10
131	d. Partner with WorkSource/One-Stop Centers	Mon 11-02-09	Fri 02-26-10
132	e. Develop charter school(s)	Mon 03-29-10	Fri 12-31-10
133	**Special Education**	**Mon 06-15-09**	**Fri 12-31-10**
134	**23. Ensure continuum of services in halls/camps**	**Wed 07-01-09**	**Fri 12-31-10**
135	a. Provide Resource Specialist Program (RSP) services	Wed 07-01-09	Fri 12-31-10
136	b. Provide Special Day Classes (SDC) services	Wed 07-01-09	Fri 12-31-10
137	c. Provide Designated Instructional Services	Wed 07-01-09	Fri 12-31-10
138	d. Provide Language Speech Specialist (LSS) services	Wed 07-01-09	Fri 12-31-10
139	**24. Ensure positive behavioral intervention plans**	**Mon 10-05-09**	**Fri 12-31-10**
140	a. Train additional juvenile DSOs in PBIP	Mon 10-05-09	Fri 12-31-10
141	b. Conduct fidelity assessment of PBIPs	Mon 01-04-10	Fri 12-31-10

Project: Compreh. Education Reform
Date: Sat 10-03-09

Page 4

Legend:
- Task Requiring Resources
- Progress
- Ongoing Task
- Completed Task
- Milestone
- Summary

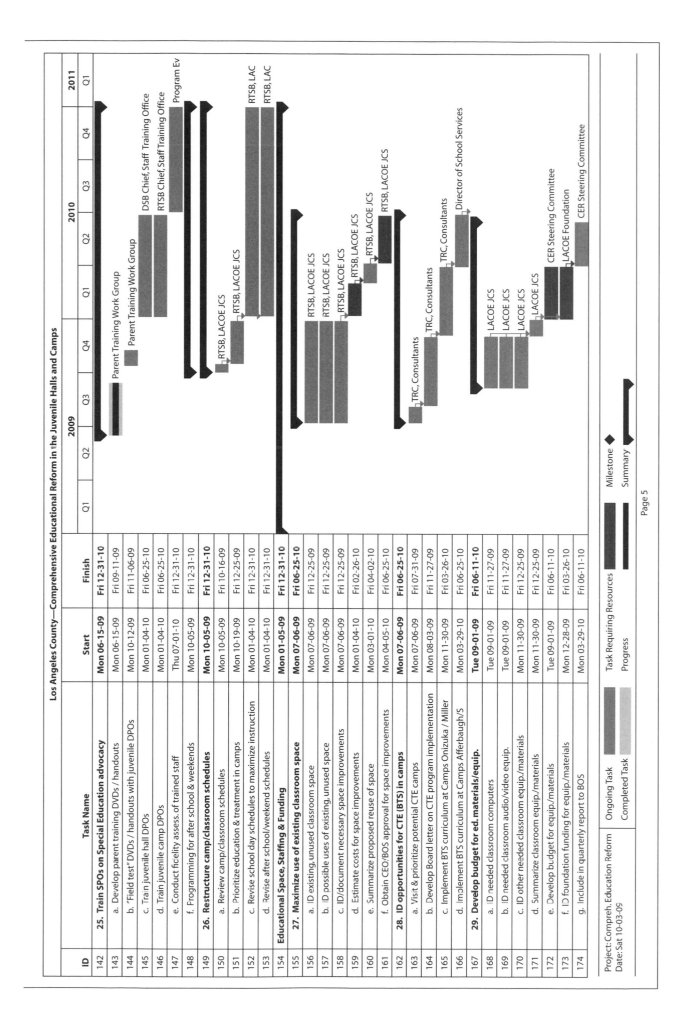

Los Angeles County—Comprehensive Educational Reform in the Juvenile Halls and Camps

ID	Task Name	Start	Finish
142	**25. Train SPOs on Special Education advocacy**	**Mon 06-15-09**	**Fri 12-31-10**
143	a. Develop parent training DVDs / handouts	Mon 06-15-09	Fri 09-11-09
144	b. "Field test" DVDs / handouts with juvenile DPOs	Mon 10-12-09	Fri 11-06-09
145	c. Train juvenile hall DPOs	Mon 01-04-10	Fri 06-25-10
146	d. Train juvenile camp DPOs	Mon 01-04-10	Fri 06-25-10
147	e. Conduct ficelity assess. of trained staff	Thu 07-01-10	Fri 12-31-10
148	f. Programming for after school & weekends	Mon 10-05-09	Fri 12-31-10
149	**26. Restructure camp/classroom schedules**	**Mon 10-05-09**	**Fri 12-31-10**
150	a. Review camp/classroom schedules	Mon 10-05-09	Fri 10-16-09
151	b. Prioritize education & treatment in camps	Mon 10-19-09	Fri 12-25-09
152	c. Revise school day schedules to maximize instruction	Mon 01-04-10	Fri 12-31-10
153	d. Revise after school/weekend schedules	Mon 01-04-10	Fri 12-31-10
154	**Educational Space, Staffing & Funding**	**Mon 01-05-09**	**Fri 12-31-10**
155	**27. Maximize use of existing classroom space**	**Mon 07-06-09**	**Fri 06-25-10**
156	a. ID existing, unused classroom space	Mon 07-06-09	Fri 12-25-09
157	b. ID possible uses of existing, unused space	Mon 07-06-09	Fri 12-25-09
158	c. ID/document necessary space improvements	Mon 07-06-09	Fri 12-25-09
159	d. Estimate costs for space improvements	Mon 01-04-10	Fri 02-26-10
160	e. Summarize proposed reuse of space	Mon 03-01-10	Fri 04-02-10
161	f. Obtain CEO/BOS approval for space improvements	Mon 04-05-10	Fri 06-25-10
162	**28. ID opportunities for CTE (BTS) in camps**	**Mon 07-06-09**	**Fri 06-25-10**
163	a. Visit & prioritize potential CTE camps	Mon 07-06-09	Fri 07-31-09
164	b. Develop Board letter on CTE program implementation	Mon 08-03-09	Fri 11-27-09
165	c. Implement BTS curriculum at Camps Onizuka / Miller	Mon 11-30-09	Fri 03-26-10
166	d. Implement BTS curriculum at Camps Afferbaugh/S	Mon 03-29-10	Fri 06-25-10
167	**29. Develop budget for ed. materials/equip.**	**Tue 09-01-09**	**Fri 06-11-10**
168	a. ID needed classroom computers	Tue 09-01-09	Fri 11-27-09
169	b. ID needed classroom audio/video equip.	Tue 09-01-09	Fri 11-27-09
170	c. ID other needed classroom equip./materials	Mon 11-30-09	Fri 12-25-09
171	d. Summarize classroom equip./materials	Mon 11-30-09	Fri 12-25-09
172	e. Develop budget for equip./materials	Tue 09-01-09	Fri 06-11-10
173	f. ID foundation funding for equip./materials	Mon 12-28-09	Fri 03-26-10
174	g. Include in quarterly report to BOS	Mon 03-29-10	Fri 06-11-10

Project: Compreh. Education Reform
Date: Sat 10-03-09

Task Requiring Resources ▬ Milestone ◆
Ongoing Task ▭ Progress ▬ Summary ▬
Completed Task ▭

Page 5

EXHIBIT 2

Microsoft Project Schedule Template (*Continued*)

Los Angeles County—Comprehensive Educational Reform in the Juvenile Halls and Camps

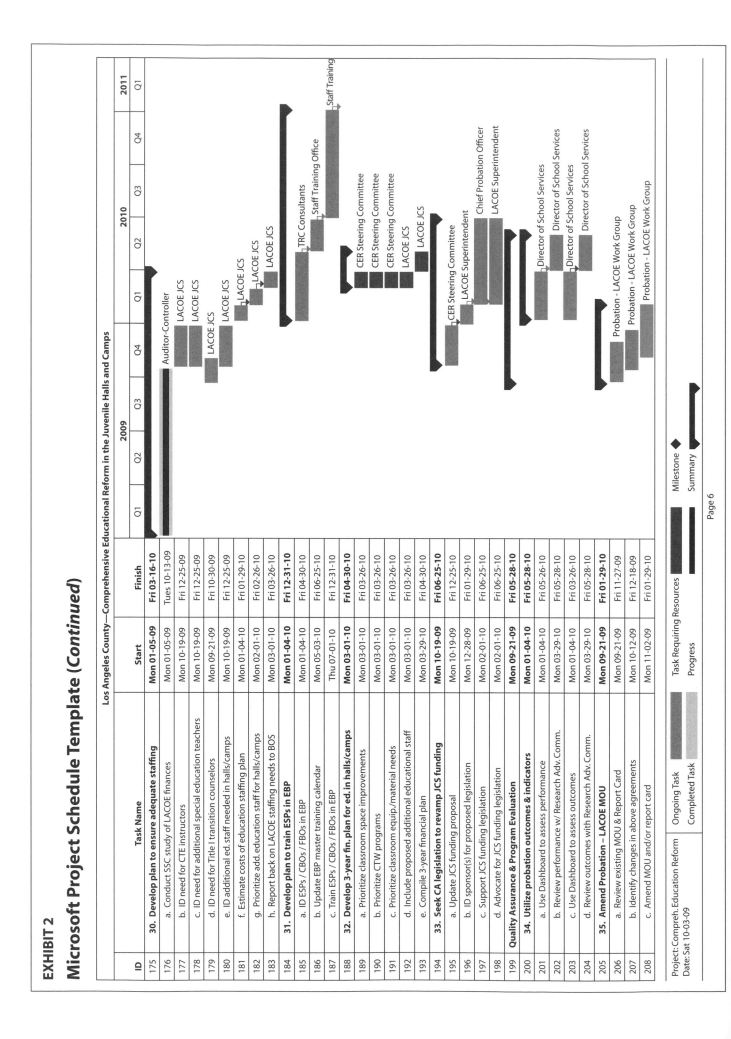

ID	Task Name	Start	Finish
175	**30. Develop plan to ensure adequate staffing**	**Mon 01-05-09**	**Fri 03-16-10**
176	a. Conduct SSC study of LACOE finances	Mon 01-05-09	Tues 10-13-09
177	b. ID need for CTE instructors	Mon 10-19-09	Fri 12-25-09
178	c. ID need for additional special education teachers	Mon 10-19-09	Fri 12-25-09
179	d. ID need for Title I transition counselors	Mon 09-21-09	Fri 10-30-09
180	e. ID additional ed. staff needed in halls/camps	Mon 10-19-09	Fri 12-25-09
181	f. Estimate costs of education staffing plan	Mon 01-04-10	Fri 01-29-10
182	g. Prioritize add. education staff for halls/camps	Mon 02-01-10	Fri 02-26-10
183	h. Report back on LACOE staffing needs to BOS	Mon 03-01-10	Fri 03-26-10
184	**31. Develop plan to train ESPs in EBP**	**Mon 01-04-10**	**Fri 12-31-10**
185	a. ID ESPs / CBOs / FBOs in EBP	Mon 01-04-10	Fri 04-30-10
186	b. Update EBP master training calendar	Mon 05-03-10	Fri 06-25-10
187	c. Train ESPs / CBOs / FBOs in EBP	Thu 07-01-10	Fri 12-31-10
188	**32. Develop 3-year fin. plan for ed. in halls/camps**	**Mon 03-01-10**	**Fri 04-30-10**
189	a. Prioritize classroom space improvements	Mon 03-01-10	Fri 03-26-10
190	b. Prioritize CTW programs	Mon 03-01-10	Fri 03-26-10
191	c. Prioritize classroom equip./material needs	Mon 03-01-10	Fri 03-26-10
192	d. Include proposed additional educational staff	Mon 03-01-10	Fri 03-26-10
193	e. Compile 3-year financial plan	Mon 03-29-10	Fri 04-30-10
194	**33. Seek CA legislation to revamp JCS funding**	**Mon 10-19-09**	**Fri 06-25-10**
195	a. Update JCS funding proposal	Mon 10-19-09	Fri 12-25-09
196	b. ID sponsor(s) for proposed legislation	Mon 12-28-09	Fri 01-29-10
197	c. Support JCS funding legislation	Mon 02-01-10	Fri 06-25-10
198	d. Advocate for JCS funding legislation	Mon 02-01-10	Fri 06-25-10
199	**Quality Assurance & Program Evaluation**	**Mon 09-21-09**	**Fri 05-28-10**
200	**34. Utilize probation outcomes & indicators**	**Mon 01-04-10**	**Fri 05-28-10**
201	a. Use Dashboard to assess performance	Mon 01-04-10	Fri 05-26-10
202	b. Review performance w/ Research Adv. Comm.	Mon 03-29-10	Fri 05-28-10
203	c. Use Dashboard to assess outcomes	Mon 01-04-10	Fri 03-26-10
204	d. Review outcomes with Research Adv. Comm.	Mon 03-29-10	Fri 05-28-10
205	**35. Amend Probation – LACOE MOU**	**Mon 09-21-09**	**Fri 01-29-10**
206	a. Review existing MOU & Report Card	Mon 09-21-09	Fri 11-27-09
207	b. Identify changes in above agreements	Mon 10-12-09	Fri 12-18-09
208	c. Amend MOU and/or report card	Mon 11-02-09	Fri 01-29-10

Project: Compreh. Education Reform
Date: Sat 10-03-09

Ongoing Task	
Completed Task	

Task Requiring Resources
Progress

Milestone ◆
Summary

Page 6

WORKSHEET 49

Strategy/Action Status Report Form

Instructions. For each strategy or action, provide an update on its status by providing the following information and responding to the following questions.

_____

Strategy/Action	**Action No.**	**Scheduled Start/Complete Dates**	**Task Leader**
_____	_____	_____ / _____	_____

Task status as of: _____

Completed: _____   Date completed: _____   Deliverable: _____

Under way: _____   Start date: _____   % Complete: _____

Anticipated completed date: _____

Comments:

    1. What has gone well?

    2. What challenges or difficulties are being encountered?

    3. What might be done to overcome the difficulties or challenges?

    4. What other strategies or actions might be needed?

    5. What other strategies or actions does this strategy or action relate to, and with what effects or consequences?

Source: _Adapted from materials developed by David Schwartz and Farnum Alston of The Resources Company._

Reassess Strategies and the Strategic Planning Process

Purpose of Step

The purpose of this final step is to review implemented strategies and the strategic planning process as a prelude to a new cycle of strategic planning. Much of the work of this phase may have occurred as part of the ongoing implementation process. However, if an organization has not engaged in strategic planning for a while, it may be useful to mark off this step as a separate one.

In this step you need to reassess strategies—and the strategic issues that prompted them—in order to decide what should be done about them. Strategies may need to be maintained, superseded by other strategies, or terminated for one reason or another.

An attempt is also made in this step to figure out whether a new round of strategic planning is warranted and, if so, what kind of strategic planning process is required and when. In doing this review, figure out how to build on the success you have had in implementation and the lessons learned. Strategic planning should build on past efforts. As organizational capacity for strategic thinking, acting, and learning increases, the strategic planning process should become easier.

Possible Desired Planning Outcomes

- Assurance that implemented strategies remain responsive to real needs and problems—and if they don't, consideration of what should be done with them based on, for example, revised mission, mandates, vision, goals, and objectives; changes in the environment; or the fact that strategies just aren't working

- Resolution of residual problems that become evident during sustained implementation

- Clarification of the strengths and weaknesses of the most recent strategic planning effort, and discussion of modifications that might be made in the next round of strategic planning

- Development of the energy, will, and ideas necessary to revise existing strategies, address important unresolved strategic issues, or undertake a full-blown strategic planning exercise

Worksheet Directions

1. At some point after implementation of the strategic plan has begun, evaluate not only the plan but the strategic planning process itself.

2. Strategy implementation is an ongoing process, not a one-time event, and the most effective way to improve it is to evaluate the success of prior efforts. Consider who should be involved in this evaluation effort (for example, key stakeholders, outside experts, strategic planning team, implementers) (Bryson, Patton, & Bowman, 2011). Use Worksheet 50.

3. On the basis of the evaluation and its findings, decide whether a new round of strategic planning is needed and what changes might be indicated. If a new round is thought necessary, fill out Worksheet 51 as a first step in charting possible improvements.

Improving Existing Strategies

Instructions. In deciding what to improve and why, it is important to be clear why changes are necessary. Is it because of a design flaw in the strategy; unintended consequences; a change in leadership, the organizational design, or the environment; or some other cause?

Strategy	Strengths	Weaknesses	Modifications That Would Improve	Summary Evaluation
				❑ Maintain ❑ Replace with a new or revised element ❑ Terminate
				❑ Maintain ❑ Replace with a new or revised element ❑ Terminate
				❑ Maintain ❑ Replace with a new or revised element ❑ Terminate
				❑ Maintain ❑ Replace with a new or revised element ❑ Terminate
				❑ Maintain ❑ Replace with a new or revised element ❑ Terminate

WORKSHEET 51

Improving the Strategic Planning Process

Instructions. In deciding what to improve and why, it is important to be clear why changes are necessary. Is it because of a design flaw in the strategic planning process; unintended consequences; a change in leadership, the organizational design, or the environment; or some other cause?

Planning Process Element	Strengths	Weaknesses	Modifications That Would Improve	Summary Evaluation
				❑ Maintain ❑ Replace with a new or revised element ❑ Terminate
				❑ Maintain ❑ Replace with a new or revised element ❑ Terminate
				❑ Maintain ❑ Replace with a new or revised element ❑ Terminate
				❑ Maintain ❑ Replace with a new or revised element ❑ Terminate
				❑ Maintain ❑ Replace with a new or revised element ❑ Terminate

Resources

A. Model Readiness Assessment Questionnaire

B. Brainstorming Guidelines

C. Snow Card Guidelines

D. Strategic Planning Workshop Equipment Checklist

E. Conference Room Setup Checklist

F. Model External Stakeholder (or Customer) Questionnaire

G. Model Internal Evaluation Questionnaire

H. Analyzing and Reporting Results of Internal and External Surveys

Model Readiness Assessment Questionnaire

This questionnaire is presented as a model only. It has been modified from actual questionnaires developed originally in 2001 by Farnum Alston and The Crescent Company and used ever since. A questionnaire of this type must be tailored to fit the organization. Every organization must choose the best approach for it to use when conducting either an internal or external assessment.

Permission is granted to use the questionnaire as long as the following credit is given:

Questionnaire adapted from proprietary materials developed by Farnum Alston and The Crescent Company, Bozeman, Montana.

Sample Hard-Copy or Electronic Letter [addressing interests of external stakeholders; write a separate letter for internal stakeholders addressing their interests]

Date:

To: XYZ Organization External Stakeholders [*or* Customers]

From: Executive Director of XYZ Organization

First, I would like to thank all of you in advance for taking the time and effort to review and complete the attached customer service questionnaire.

A few years ago, XYZ developed a strategic plan to

- Update our mission, vision, and value statements and also our goals, objectives, and strategies for accomplishing our mission of providing services that are high quality, timely, fiscally responsible, and convenient for our stakeholders [*or* customers]—you, the organizations that we serve.

- Guide preparation of action plans and timetables to implement our strategies.

- Develop performance indicators and a process for measuring customer service and organizational effectiveness and efficiency.

- Establish a process and key milestones to be used by XYZ management in monitoring implementation of the strategic plan.

This questionnaire is a follow-up opportunity for you to provide our organization with some feedback on implementation of our strategies and to help us decide what to do next. It is another chance to raise issues and suggestions for improvement. All ideas will be considered.

If you have any questions about completing the questionnaire, please contact [*insert full contact details*].

The ABC Company (whom we have hired to conduct this survey) will keep all questionnaires confidential and the compiled results we receive will not disclose individual responses.

To simplify and speed up the process for you, you may submit the questionnaire electronically. Please e-mail the completed questionnaire as an attachment to [*insert full contact details*]. [*Or* To simplify and speed up the process for you, you may respond to an electronic online survey available at (*insert URL*)].

Please return your responses no later than [*insert date*].

Thank you again for your participation.

Readiness Assessment Questionnaire

My organization or unit is: _____

My program area is: _____

My role is: _____

Instructions for Completion

There are no "right" or "wrong" answers. For each question in this questionnaire, please *circle* the number from 1 to 5 that most closely reflects how you feel about the two given statements.

Please be candid in your responses, and draw on your most recent experience in the last two years.

Readiness Assessment Questions

Mission

1.

1	2	3	4	5

As an organization [*or* group] we have a clear mission.

As an organization [*or* group] we do not have a clear mission.

2.

1	2	3	4	5

As an organization all our work is informed by our mission.

We pay little attention to our mission on a day-to-day basis.

Stakeholders

3.

1	2	3	4	5

We are unclear about who our key stakeholders are and what matters to them.

We know who our key stakeholders are and what matters to them.

4.

1	2	3	4	5

We engage with key stakeholders in effective ways to facilitate our work.

We do not spend much time engaging key stakeholders.

Leadership

5.

1	2	3	4	5

Our leadership team is clearly focused.

Our leadership team is not clearly focused.

6.

1	2	3	4	5

There is not a high level of trust among the leadership team.

There is a high level of trust among the leadership team.

7.

1	2	3	4	5

I personally have a strong sense of urgency to move our organization ahead.

I personally feel little urgency to move our organization ahead.

Communication and Information Technology

8.

1	2	3	4	5

We have effective two-way communications both in and out of the organization [or group].

Our two-way communications both in and out of the organization [or group] are very often not what they should be.

9.

1	2	3	4	5

We do not have the information technology we need to do the work (including appropriate Web 2.0 and higher technologies).

We have more than adequate information technology needed to do the work (including appropriate Web 2.0 and higher technologies).

Deliberation and Decision Making

10.

1	2	3	4	5

Deliberation and dialogue about important matters are encouraged in our organization.

We do not deliberate or engage in dialogue about important matters in this organization.

11.

1	2	3	4	5

We do not make much use of data or analysis when making important decisions.

We make extensive use of data and analysis to make important decisions.

12.

1	2	3	4	5

We act quickly to address important issues.

We often let important matters slide until they get quite serious before addressing them.

Budgeting and Resources

13.

1	2	3	4	5

We suffer from chronic resource shortages.

We always have or find the resources needed to get the job done.

Structure and Processes

14.

1	2	3	4	5

There is effective cross-organizational cooperation.

Units do not work well with one another.

15.

1	2	3	4	5

There are adequate incentives to encourage working together.

There are few incentives for working together.

16.

1	2	3	4	5

There is a merit-based system of rewards and recognition.

There is not an effective merit-based system of rewards and recognition.

17.

1	2	3	4	5

Our organization's structure is flexible to accommodate change.

Our organization's structure is rigid and resists change.

Culture

18.

1	2	3	4	5

We work independently.

We work as a team.

19.

1	2	3	4	5

Risk taking is encouraged.

Risk taking is not encouraged.

20.

1	2	3	4	5

I am open to change.

I see little reason to change the way I am working.

21.

1	2	3	4	5

I feel valued as an employee.

I am not valued as an employee.

22.

1	2	3	4	5

We have a strong work ethic as an organization [or group].

We lack a strong work ethic as an organization [or group].

Implementation

23.

1	2	3	4	5

Our day-to-day work gets in the way of implementing major changes.

We are able to do both our day-to-day work and accommodate major changes.

24.

1	2	3	4	5

We are not a performance-driven organization.

We are a performance-driven organization.

25.

1	2	3	4	5

We are very good at managing projects on time and on budget.

We have trouble finishing projects.

Any final comments?

Analyzing and Reporting Results

The results of the questionnaire can be tabulated by the organization as a whole or by groups or specific stakeholders.

Analyzing Single Questions

A. Question 13.

1	2 (Av 2.3)	3	4	5
We suffer from chronic resource shortages.		We always have or find the resources needed to get the job done.		

The average answer here might be 2.3, meaning "we often suffer from resources shortages." Thus resource development or use may be a strategic issue that will need to be addressed; otherwise, plan implementation is likely to suffer.

B. Question 21.

1	2 (Mgt 2.2)	3 (Emp 3.8)	4	5
I feel valued as an employee.		I am not valued as an employee.		

In this example, two groups have responded quite differently. Managers' (Mgt) average answer is 2.2, whereas other employees' (Emp) average answer is 3.8. These two groups thus experience the organization very differently. Managers feel more valued and other employees feel less valued. The sources of this difference need to be explored, and the findings may lead to the identification of major strategic issues and implications for the design of the strategic planning process.

C. Question 8.

1	2 (Org 2.1)	3	4 (Ext 4.3)	5
We have effective two-way communications both in and out of the organization [or group].		Our two-way communications both in and out of the organization [or group] are very often not what they should be.		

In this example as well, organizational members' (Org) average score of 2.1 indicate that they think two-way communications are far more effective than do external stakeholders (Ext), whose average score of 4.3 indicates some serious problems with externally oriented two-way communications. Again, there are likely to be some important implications for the strategic planning process and for strategic issues that need to be addressed.

Interpreting Total Scores Across All Questions

In order to come up with a total score for the organization as a whole, you will first have to reverse score several questions, so that on all scales a score of 5 indicates the organization is in very good condition with regard to the particular item. (On this survey, questions 1, 2, 4, 5, 7, 8, 10, 12, 14, 15, 16, 17, 19, 20, 21, and 25 need to be reverse scored.)

Once the reverse scoring is complete, add up all the scores. There are twenty-five questions, so the highest possible score is 125.

Total Score	Interpretation
101–125	The organization is generally in very good shape and probably just needs some fine-tuning to address some specific issues. Alternatively, the organization may be poised to pursue a full-blown effort to go to the next level.
75–100	The organization has some significant issues that are keeping it from fulfilling its full potential. Any really serious issues should be the focus of a targeted strategic planning effort to address them. These issues might be addressed as part of a larger overall strategic planning effort, but they may well need to be addressed first.
50–74	The organization faces very serious issues. Scores indicate either mediocrity across the board or else some specific issues meriting serious attention. If the organization is to survive, a concerted effort will be needed to address these issues. Organizational transformation of some sort is needed (perhaps over a significant time period) and will require impressive leadership efforts to achieve. Decide whether the leadership group (broadly defined) is up to the effort, the leadership group is in need of development, or new leadership is required.
25–49	The organization is in trouble. The scores indicate either barely adequate performance across the board or some possible areas of strength but other major areas in need of drastic improvement. Consider addressing the most important of these issues prior to engaging in a full-blown strategic planning effort. Strong leadership of many kinds will be needed if the organization is to change enough to ensure survival.
0–24	The organization is in quite serious trouble. A slow (or not so slow) death is under way and may be hastened by any significant shock. Try to fix one or a few of the serious issues to assess whether it is worth the effort to try to revive the organization.

The interpretation of a readiness survey illuminates an important paradox of strategic planning: it is least needed where it is most likely to work—that is, in organizations that score in the upper part of the possible range—and most needed where it is least likely to work—that is, in organizations that score in the lower part of the range. More explicitly, organizations with low scores are unlikely to have the leadership and resources necessary to address the many issues they face, so the chances that everything will come together in an adequate way for them are not high (Bryson, 2011). Nonetheless, the authors of this workbook have seen dramatic turnarounds, so success, even though hardly assured, is not out of the question.

Brainstorming Guidelines

Brainstorming is a way of producing a large quantity of ideas so that the likelihood of coming up with at least one *high-quality* idea is increased. As Nobel laureate Linus Pauling once said, "The best way to have a good idea is to have a lot of ideas." Guidelines for brainstorming are as follows:

1. Agree to participate in a brainstorming exercise.

2. Appoint a facilitator and a note taker.

3. Focus on a *single* problem or issue. Don't skip around to various problems or try to brainstorm answers to a complex, multiple-factor problem.

4. Have people record their responses to the problem or issue silently and individually on a sheet of scratch paper.

5. Go around the room in round-robin fashion. In each round each individual should offer, in turn, one idea in response to the problem or issue. The recorder should record all ideas in the speaker's own words.

6. Do not criticize or evaluate any of the ideas put forward; they are simply placed before the group and recorded.

7. Be open to hearing some wild ideas in the spontaneity that evolves when the group suspends judgment. Practical considerations are not important at this point. The session is meant to be freewheeling.

8. Emphasize that the quantity of ideas counts, not their quality. All ideas should be expressed, and none should be screened out by any participant. A great number of ideas will increase the likelihood of the group's discovering good ones.

9. Build on the ideas of other group members when possible. Pool people's creativity. Everyone should be free to build onto any idea and to make interesting amalgams from the various suggestions.

10. Foster a congenial, relaxed, cooperative atmosphere.

11. Make sure that all members, no matter how shy and reluctant to contribute, get their ideas heard.

12. Record *all* ideas.

Snow Card Guidelines

The snow card (or affinity diagram) process starts with brainstorming and then goes beyond it by having participants organize the brainstormed ideas into clusters that share a common theme or subject matter. Guidelines for engaging in the snow card process are as follows:

1. Bring a single problem or issue into the group.

2. Have individuals in the group brainstorm as many ideas as possible and record them on individual worksheets.

3. Ask individuals to pick out their five "best items" and to transcribe each one onto its own *snow card*—half of an 8-1/2 by 11 inch sheet of paper, a 5 by 7 inch card, or a large Post-it note.

4. Shuffle the cards; then tape them to a wall in categories. The group should determine the categories after reviewing several of the items. The resulting clusters of cards may resemble a "blizzard" of ideas—hence the term *snow cards*.

5. Establish subcategories as needed.

6. Once all items are on the wall and included in a category, rearrange and tinker with the categories until they make the most sense.

7. Create a label for each category and subcategory on a separate snow card.

8. When finished, take down the cards in their categories and have all the ideas typed up and distributed to the group.

Source: *Based on a technique developed by Richard B. Duke of the University of Michigan and by the Institute of Cultural Affairs (Spencer, 1996).*

Resource D

Strategic Planning Workshop Equipment Checklist

- ❑ Strategic planning process outlines
- ❑ Strategic planning workbooks (*Creating Your Strategic Plan*)
- ❑ Strategic planning books (Bryson, 2011)
- ❑ Strategic planning DVDs, podcasts, Facebook segments, and so forth
- ❑ Sample strategic plans
- ❑ Snow cards (35 per person) (see Resource C)
- ❑ Bullet-tipped flipchart marking pens, for writing on flipcharts and snow cards (dark colors)
- ❑ Flipcharts and easels (two or more)
- ❑ Whiteboard markers (various colors)
- ❑ Masking tape
- ❑ Drafting tape
- ❑ 3/4 inch stick-on dots in different colors
- ❑ Post-it notes in various sizes and colors
- ❑ Screen
- ❑ Video monitor
- ❑ DVD player
- ❑ Laptop computer and printer
- ❑ LCD projector
- ❑ Overhead projector (including spare bulb)
- ❑ Blank transparencies
- ❑ Nonpermanent marking pens for transparencies

❏ CD player or equivalent device
❏ Extension cords and power strips
❏ Digital camera (or still camera, film, and flash attachment) and access to one-hour photo shop
❏ Access to photocopy machine
❏ Secretarial support

Conference Room Setup Checklist

❑ Comfortable setting, free of distractions and phones (cell phones and other devices turned off)

❑ Plenty of space to move around

❑ Good lighting and ventilation

❑ Small tables that can be moved out of the way

❑ Comfortable, movable chairs

❑ Adequate breakout area(s)

❑ Substantial unbroken wall spaces on which flipchart sheets or snow cards can be taped

❑ Adequate electrical outlets

❑ Extension cords and power strips

❑ High-speed Internet connection

❑ Coffee/tea/soft drinks/mineral water

❑ Bread/rolls

❑ Fresh fruit

❑ Hard candies

❑ Adequate restroom facilities

❑ Handicapped accessible (including restroom facilities)

Model External Stakeholder (or Customer) Questionnaire

This questionnaire is presented as a model only. It has been modified from actual questionnaires developed originally in 2001 by Farnum Alston and The Crescent Company and used ever since. A questionnaire of this type must be tailored to fit the organization. Every organization must choose the best approach for it to use when conducting an external assessment.

Permission is granted to use the questionnaire as long as the following credit is given:

Questionnaire adapted from proprietary materials developed by Farnum Alston and The Crescent Company, Bozeman, Montana.

Sample Letter

Date:

To: XYZ Organization Stakeholders [*or* Customers]

From: Executive Director of XYZ Organization

First, I would like to thank all of you in advance for taking the time and effort to review and complete the attached customer service questionnaire.

A few years ago, XYZ developed a strategic plan to

- Update our mission, vision, and value statements and also our goals, objectives, and strategies for accomplishing our mission of providing services that are high quality, on time, fiscally responsible, and convenient for our stakeholders [*or* customers]—you, the organizations that we serve.

- Develop an action plan and timetable to implement our strategies.

- Develop performance indicators and a process for measuring customer service and organizational effectiveness and efficiency.

- Establish a process and key milestones to be used by XYZ management in monitoring implementation of the strategic plan.

This questionnaire is a follow-up opportunity for you to provide our organization with some feedback on implementation of our strategies. It is another chance to raise service improvement issues and suggestions. All ideas will be considered.

If you have any questions about completing the questionnaire, please contact [*insert contact details*].

The ABC Company (whom we have hired to conduct this survey) will keep all questionnaires confidential and the compiled results we receive will not disclose individual responses.

To simplify and speed up the process for you, you may submit the questionnaire electronically. Please e-mail the completed questionnaire as an attachment to [*insert contact details*]. [*Or* To simplify and speed up the process for you, you may respond to an electronic online survey available at (*insert URL*)].

Please return your responses no later than [*insert date*].

Thank you again for your participation.

External Customer Questionnaire

Please complete the following information:

My organization is: _____

My program area is: _____

Instructions for Completion

There are no "right" or "wrong" answers.

1. For each question in this questionnaire, please *circle* the number from 1 to 10 that most closely reflects how you feel about the two given statements.

2. If a set of statements does not apply to your position in the Organization, please mark the NA (no response) blank.

Please be candid in your responses, and draw on your most recent experience in the last two years.

Sample Question

Resources

| 1 | 2 | 3 | 4 | 5 | 6 | 7 | ⑧ | 9 | 10 | NA____ |

Resources *are* likely to increase in the next five years.

Resources *are not* likely to increase in the next five years.

Circling 1 would indicate strong agreement with the statement on the left that resources are likely to increase in the next five years.

Circling 10 would indicate strong agreement with the statement on the right that resources are not likely to increase in the next five years.

Circling 8 would indicate moderate agreement with the statement on the right, and so forth.

If you have any questions about completing the questionnaire, please contact Dr. Jane Smith of the ABC Company at [*insert contact details*].

I. Use and Assessment of XYZ Organization's Services

A. Use of XYZ Services

Please indicate the level of XYZ services used by your organization. Mark NA for XYZ services not used by your organization. [*Add questions to this section to address use of each major service.*]

Level of use of XYZ's XXX Service

1   2   3   4   5   6   7   8   9   10   NA____

Our organization is a relatively small user of XYZ's XXX service.   Our organization is a relatively large user of XYZ's XXX service.

B. Timeliness of XYZ Services Used by Your Organization

Please rate the timeliness of XYZ services used by your organization. Mark NA for XYZ services not used by your organization. [*Add questions to this section to address timeliness of each major service.*]

Timeliness of XYZ's XXX Service

1   2   3   4   5   6   7   8   9   10   NA____

XYZ's XXX service is not very timely.   XYZ's XXX service is very timely.

C. Quality of XYZ Services Used by Your Organization

Please rate the quality of XYZ services used by your organization. Mark NA for XYZ services not used by your organization. [*Add questions to this section to address the quality of each major service.*]

Quality of XYZ's XXX Service

1   2   3   4   5   6   7   8   9   10   NA____

The quality of XYZ's XXX service needs improvement.   The quality of XYZ's XXX service is excellent.

D. Cost of XYZ Services Used by Your Organization

Please rate the cost of XYZ services used by your organization. Mark NA for XYZ services not used by your organization. [*Add questions to this section to address the cost of each major service.*]

Cost of XYZ's XXX Service

1   2   3   4   5   6   7   8   9   10   NA____

The cost of XYZ's XXX service is appropriate.   The cost of XYZ's XXX service is too high.

Comments

Please comment below on your organization's use of XYZ services.

You may also mention items not specifically addressed in the survey questions, or expand on your responses to particular survey items.

If you prefer, you can write out your answers to this and other comment sections in a separate file titled "Comments" [*or in the online survey*, in a text box for comments] or on separate pieces of paper. Be sure to attach this separate file to your questionnaire e-mail or enclose the papers with the questionnaire when it is returned by hand or mail.

Please feel free to comment on why your organization does or does not use certain XYZ services. Also feel free to suggest other services that you would like to see XYZ provide to your organization.

II. General Observations About XYZ Organization

1. Relevancy of the Mission and Vision

   1   2   3   4   5   6   7   8   9   10   NA____

   XYZ's mission and vision are relevant
   and clear.

   XYZ's mission and vision are outdated or
   unclear.

2. Service Versus Compliance

   1   2   3   4   5   6   7   8   9   10   NA____

   XYZ seems guided by its mission and
   vision.

   In its daily activities XYZ seems oriented
   toward day-to-day procedures.

3. Knowledge of Stakeholders

   1   2   3   4   5   6   7   8   9   10   NA____

   XYZ understands us and our needs.

   XYZ does not have a clear understanding
   of our organization or our business.

4. Environmental Scanning

   1   2   3   4   5   6   7   8   9   10   NA____

   XYZ seems to routinely monitor
   changes in its work environment.

   XYZ does not seem to routinely monitor
   changes in its work environment.

5. Attitude Toward Change

   1   2   3   4   5   6   7   8   9   10   NA____

   Overall, XYZ seems to see change as
   an opportunity.

   Overall, XYZ tends to avoid change or to
   view it as high risk.

6. Information Technology

   1   2   3   4   5   6   7   8   9   10   NA____

   XYZ effectively uses technology in
   the management of the organization.

   XYZ makes ineffective use of technology
   in its management.

7. Decision-Making Clarity

   1   2   3   4   5   6   7   8   9   10   NA____

   XYZ's decision-making processes are
   poorly defined.

   XYZ's decision-making processes are
   clearly defined.

8. Decision-Making Consistency

| 1 | 2 | 3 | 4 | 5 | 6 | 7 | 8 | 9 | 10 | NA____ |

XYZ's decision-making processes seem to be inconsistently followed.

XYZ's decision-making processes seem to be consistently followed.

9. Information

| 1 | 2 | 3 | 4 | 5 | 6 | 7 | 8 | 9 | 10 | NA____ |

In XYZ, information seems to be viewed as a resource and is generally shared.

In XYZ, information seems to be used as a basis for power and is generally tightly controlled.

10. Synergy

| 1 | 2 | 3 | 4 | 5 | 6 | 7 | 8 | 9 | 10 | NA____ |

People in XYZ seem willing and able to work collaboratively, openly, and respectfully with one another.

People in XYZ seem unwilling or unable to work collaboratively, openly, or respectfully with one another.

11. External Communications

| 1 | 2 | 3 | 4 | 5 | 6 | 7 | 8 | 9 | 10 | NA____ |

XYZ's communications to us are random and provide confused or inconsistent messages.

XYZ's communications to us are carefully targeted and provide clear and consistent messages.

12. Priorities

| 1 | 2 | 3 | 4 | 5 | 6 | 7 | 8 | 9 | 10 | NA____ |

XYZ clearly defines its priorities to us.

XYZ does not clearly define its priorities to us.

13. Delegation of Authority

| 1 | 2 | 3 | 4 | 5 | 6 | 7 | 8 | 9 | 10 | NA____ |

Decision making and control seem delegated to the lowest appropriate levels in XYZ.

Decision making and control seem retained at inappropriately high levels in XYZ.

14. Recognition

1   2   3   4   5   6   7   8   9   10   NA____

XYZ acknowledges actions that
support its strategies and goals.

XYZ does not acknowledge actions that
support its strategies and goals.

15. Creativity

1   2   3   4   5   6   7   8   9   10   NA____

Individuals in XYZ seem encouraged to develop new ideas and to
improve operational efficiency and
effectiveness.

Individuals in XYZ seem discouraged from
developing new ideas or from improving
operational efficiency and effectiveness.

16. Risk Taking

1   2   3   4   5   6   7   8   9   10   NA____

XYZ managers discourage risk taking
in support of organizational mission
and strategies.

XYZ managers encourage risk taking in
support of organizational mission and
strategies.

17. Cross-Departmental or Cross-Functional Work

1   2   3   4   5   6   7   8   9   10   NA____

Individuals seem encouraged to work
across departmental and functional
lines to achieve their goals.

Individuals are not encouraged to work
across departmental and functional lines.

18. Roles and Responsibilities

1   2   3   4   5   6   7   8   9   10   NA____

Roles and responsibilities are clear
and appropriate in XYZ.

Roles and responsibilities are ambiguous
in XYZ.

19. Teamwork

1   2   3   4   5   6   7   8   9   10   NA____

XYZ's managers work effectively
together as a team.

XYZ's managers do not work effectively
together as a team.

20. Accountability

    1   2   3   4   5   6   7   8   9   10   NA____

    Individuals in XYZ seem to be held   Individuals in XYZ seem not to be held
    accountable.   accountable.

21. Organizational Knowledge

    1   2   3   4   5   6   7   8   9   10   NA____

    The purpose and function of each   The purpose and function of each work-
    workgroup within XYZ is effectively   group within XYZ is not known and not
    communicated and understood.   understood.

22. Discussion Forums

    1   2   3   4   5   6   7   8   9   10   NA____

    XYZ provides forums in which we can   XYZ does not provide any occasions or
    discuss issues of concern to us.   settings in which we can discuss issues of
                                                concern to us.

23. Customer Service

    1   2   3   4   5   6   7   8   9   10   NA____

    XYZ knows its customers and XYZ is a   XYZ does not know its customers
    customer-service organization.   and XYZ is not a customer-service
                                                organization.

24. Culture

    1   2   3   4   5   6   7   8   9   10   NA____

    XYZ's culture fosters a commitment   XYZ's culture diverts the organization
    to the organization's mission and the   from its mission and the satisfaction of its
    satisfaction of its key stakeholders.   key stakeholders.

III. Open Questions

A. What would you identify as XYZ's most important *strengths*?

1.

2.

3.

4.

5.

B. What would you identify as XYZ's most important *weaknesses*?

1.

2.

3.

4.

5.

C. If you could change anything about XYZ, what would it be?

1.

2.

3.

4.

5.

Thank you for your effort in completing this questionnaire.

Model Internal Evaluation Questionnaire

This questionnaire is presented as a model only. It has been modified from actual questionnaires developed originally in 2001 by Farnum Alston and The Crescent Company and used ever since. A questionnaire of this type must be tailored to fit the organization. Every organization must choose the best approach for it to use when conducting an external assessment.

Permission is granted to use the questionnaire as long as the following credit is given:

Questionnaire adapted from proprietary materials developed by Farnum Alston and The Crescent Company, Bozeman, Montana.

Confidential Material

Date:_____

To: All Staff

From: General Manager [*or* Director *or* Process Champion]

First, I would like to thank all of you in advance for taking the time and effort to review and complete the attached questionnaire.

This questionnaire is an opportunity for you to provide feedback on XYZ. It is also your chance to raise stakeholder or customer service improvement issues and suggestions. All ideas will be considered and the information will be shared with staff at a _____ Meeting to be held _____ in the _____.

ABC Company (our external consultant) will keep all questionnaires confidential and the compiled results we receive will not disclose individual responses.

To simplify and speed up the process for you, you may submit the questionnaire electronically. Please e-mail the completed questionnaire as an attachment to [*insert full contact details*]. [*Or* To simplify and speed up the process for you, you may respond to an electronic online survey available at (*insert URL*)].

Your completed questionnaires can also be dropped into the sealed collection boxes provided in the lobby. _____ will pick up the drop boxes. You may also mail your response directly to _____.

We need your responses returned by _____.

Thank you again for your participation.

Internal Evaluation Questionnaire

Please complete the following information:

My XYZ department is: _____

My job category is: _____ Manager/Supervisor (including Technical Services)

_____ Professional/Technician/Craft/ Trade (including custodians, vehicle maintenance workers)

_____ Office Support (including clerical, IS, messengers)

Instructions for Completion

There are no "right" or "wrong" answers.

1. For each question in this questionnaire, please *circle* the number from 1 to 10 that most closely reflects how you feel about the two given statements.

2. If a set of statements does not apply to your position in XYZ, please mark the NA (no response) blank.

Please be candid in your responses and draw on your most recent experiences in the last two years.

Sample Question

Resources

1   2   3   4   5   6   7   (8)   9   10   NA____

Resources *are* likely to increase in the next five years.   Resources *are not* likely to increase in the next five years.

Circling 1 would indicate strong agreement with the statement on the left that resources are likely to increase in the next five years.

Circling 10 would indicate strong agreement with the statement on the right that resources are not likely to increase in the next five years.

Circling 8 would indicate moderate agreement with the statement on the right, and so forth.

If you have any questions, please contact Dr. Jane Smith of the ABC Company at [*insert contact details*].

I. Mission, Vision, and the Organization's Environment

Successful performance organizations possess a clear understanding of their mandates. They also have established an organizational mission and vision and have communicated it to their employees and stakeholders.

- *Vision* is an image of XYZ's desired future state. XYZ's vision is *to achieve the greatest value for our stakeholders (or customers) through innovative, proactive, and convenient service solutions.*

- *Mission* is XYZ's overriding purpose. Mission provides a reason for stakeholders to support XYZ. The mission of XYZ is *to provide high-quality services that are on time, fiscally responsible, and convenient for our stakeholders* [or *customers*].

- *Environment* is used in this questionnaire to describe the context in which XYZ pursues its mission and vision. The *external environment* can present both opportunities and challenges (or threats), while the *internal environment* provides strengths on which we can draw and weaknesses we must overcome or minimize.

- *Stakeholders* refers to both internal and external people, groups, and organizations that affect XYZ and are in turn affected by XYZ. They include all XYZ employees, unions, and clients or consumers, also the legislature, some agencies, some special interest groups, the media, our regulated industry, and so forth.

- *Environmental scanning* is the tracking and analysis of factors and trends that do or could affect XYZ, that is, marketplace and business trends, use of resources, technological change, new regulations and changes, and so forth.

Questions

1. Relevance of XYZ's Mission and Vision Statements

   1   2   3   4   5   6   7   8   9   10   NA____

   Our XYZ mission and vision statements are relevant; they accurately reflect organizational aspirations and environmental realities.

   Our XYZ mission and vision statements are outdated; they no longer reflect organizational aspirations and environmental realities.

2. Effectiveness of Mission and Vision

   1   2   3   4   5   6   7   8   9   10   NA____

   Individuals and units work together in support of a common XYZ mission and vision.

   Individuals and units work toward fulfilling disparate missions and visions.

3. Service Versus Compliance

    1   2   3   4   5   6   7   8   9   10   NA____

    In our daily activities we are guided   In our daily activities we are oriented
    by XYZ's mission and vision.   toward day-to-day compliance with poli-
                                    cies and procedures.

4. Knowledge of Stakeholders

    1   2   3   4   5   6   7   8   9   10   NA____

    We understand our current and   We do not have a clear understanding of
    potential stakeholders.   our current or potential stakeholders.

5. Environmental Scanning

    1   2   3   4   5   6   7   8   9   10   NA____

    We routinely monitor changes in our   We do not routinely monitor changes in
    work environment that could affect   our work environment that may affect
    XYZ, and we assess potential losses or   XYZ.
    reduction in services and potential
    opportunities.

6. Response to the Environment

    1   2   3   4   5   6   7   8   9   10   NA____

    We work to define our future within   We address changing factors in the
    the context of changing factors in the   environment only when they begin to
    environment; we respond proactively   be felt; we respond reactively to our
    to our environment.   environment.

7. Attitude Toward Change

    1   2   3   4   5   6   7   8   9   10   NA____

    Overall, we respond to change by   Overall, we tend to avoid change or to
    seeing opportunities.   view it as high risk.

Comments

Please comment below on XYZ's Mission and Vision.

You may also mention items not specifically addressed in the questionnaire questions or expand on your responses to particular questionnaire items.

If you prefer you can write out your answers to this and other comment sections in a separate file titled "Comments" [*or in the online survey*, in a text box for comments] or on separate pieces of paper. Be sure to attach this separate file to your questionnaire e-mail or to enclose the papers with the questionnaire when it is returned by hand or mail.

II. Budget, Human Resources, and Information Technology

This section of the questionnaire focuses on the management of budgets, human resources, and information technology. Successful organizations and managers achieve their mission and attain their vision by effectively managing their resources.

Questions

8. Internal Budgeting Process

   1   2   3   4   5   6   7   8   9   10   NA____

   Our budgeting process is clearly defined, communicated, and consistently followed.

   Our budgeting process is not clearly defined, communicated, or consistently followed.

9. Allocation of Staff and Funds

   1   2   3   4   5   6   7   8   9   10   NA____

   Our staff and dollars are clearly linked to XYZ's mission and priorities.

   Our staff and dollars are not linked to XYZ's mission and priorities.

10. Information Technology

    1   2   3   4   5   6   7   8   9   10   NA____

    We use technology effectively in managing XYZ's resources and pursuing its mission.

    We make ineffective use of information technology in managing XYZ's resources and pursuing its mission.

11. Management Respect

    1   2   3   4   5   6   7   8   9   10   NA____

    I generally feel that management respects me as a person and values the work I do.

    I generally feel that management does not respect me enough or value the work I do.

12. Supervisor Respect

    1   2   3   4   5   6   7   8   9   10   NA____

    I generally feel that my supervisor respects me as a person and values the work I do.

    I generally feel that my supervisor does not respect me enough or value the work I do.

13. Performance Measures

1	2	3	4	5	6	7	8	9	10	NA____

Clear performance measures exist that link my work to XYZ's mission and goals.

Clear performance measures that link my work to XYZ's mission and goals do not exist.

14. Job Satisfaction

1	2	3	4	5	6	7	8	9	10	NA____

In general, I am not satisfied with my job.

In general, I am satisfied with my job.

15. Advancement

1	2	3	4	5	6	7	8	9	10	NA____

There is a lack of opportunities for advancement within XYZ.

There are adequate opportunities for advancement within XYZ.

16. Empowerment

1	2	3	4	5	6	7	8	9	10	NA____

I feel empowered to work effectively and efficiently in XYZ.

I do not feel empowered to work effectively and efficiently in XYZ.

17. Compensation

1	2	3	4	5	6	7	8	9	10	NA____

My level of compensation is appropriate for my work.

My level of compensation is not appropriate for my work.

Comments

Please comment on any of XYZ's significant strengths or weaknesses in the areas of budgets, human resources, and information technology. You may address issues not specifically raised in the questionnaire questions or expand on your responses to particular questionnaire items. As before, you may do this electronically or on paper, being sure to return the comments with your questionnaire.

III. Communications

This section examines the flow of information within XYZ. Successful organizations transmit clear messages, have well-developed communication networks, and have adequate forums to promote discussion and dialogue.

- *Messages* are clear, concise, and targeted toward specific stakeholders, and designed to produce specific responses.
- *Communication networks* effectively convey information to both internal and external stakeholders.
- *Forums* provide the occasions and settings for appropriate discussion and dialogue.

Questions

18. Decision-Making Process Clarity

    1   2   3   4   5   6   7   8   9   10   NA____

    XYZ's decision-making processes are poorly defined.

    XYZ's decision-making processes are clearly defined.

19. Decision-Making Process Consistency

    1   2   3   4   5   6   7   8   9   10   NA____

    XYZ's decision-making processes are inconsistently followed.

    XYZ's decision-making processes are consistently followed.

20. Information

    1   2   3   4   5   6   7   8   9   10   NA____

    In XYZ, information is viewed as a resource and is generally shared.

    In XYZ, information is used as a basis for power and is generally tightly controlled.

21. Synergy

    1   2   3   4   5   6   7   8   9   10   NA____

    In general, people are willing and able to work collaboratively, openly, and respectfully with one another.

    In general, people are unwilling or unable to work collaboratively, openly, or respectfully with one another.

22. Black Holes

    1   2   3   4   5   6   7   8   9   10   NA____

    We have some organizational "black   Information is communicated
    holes" where information becomes   throughout XYZ in a clear, consistent,
    distorted, inconsistent, or stalled.   and timely manner.

23. Internal Communications

    1   2   3   4   5   6   7   8   9   10   NA____

    Our internal communications provide   Our internal communications are
    confused and inconsistent messages.   carefully done and very effective.

24. External Communications

    1   2   3   4   5   6   7   8   9   10   NA____

    Our communications to our   Our communications to customers are
    customers are random and provide   carefully targeted and provide a clear
    confused or inconsistent messages.   and consistent message.

25. Discussion Forums

    1   2   3   4   5   6   7   8   9   10   NA____

    XYZ provides forums in which we can   XYZ does not provide any occasions or
    discuss issues of concern to us.   settings in which we can discuss issues
                                                                of concern to us.

Comments

Please comment on any significant XYZ strengths or weaknesses in the area of communications. You may address issues not specifically raised in the questionnaire questions or expand on your responses to particular questionnaire items. As before, you may do this electronically or on paper, being sure to return the comments with your questionnaire.

IV. Leadership, Management, Organization, and Culture

This section examines various aspects of leadership, management, organization, and culture. Successful organizations enjoy inspirational leadership, competent management, and organize themselves in strategic ways.

- *Leadership* may be defined as making sure that XYZ is doing the right things.
- *Management* may be defined as making sure that those things are being done right.
- The *organization* is the purposeful structure of relationships *across and down in XYZ* in order to carry out specific strategies and initiatives.

Questions

26. Senior Administrative Leadership (XYZ Deputy Director and above)

    1   2   3   4   5   6   7   8   9   10   NA____

    The senior administrator spends sufficient time on leadership activities.

    The senior administrator spends too little time providing leadership.

27. Midlevel Management

    1   2   3   4   5   6   7   8   9   10   NA____

    Midlevel administrators spend sufficient time on management.

    Midlevel administrators spend too little time on management activities.

28. XYZ Priorities

    1   2   3   4   5   6   7   8   9   10   NA____

    XYZ clearly defines its priorities.

    XYZ does not clearly define its priorities.

29. Delegation of Authority

    1   2   3   4   5   6   7   8   9   10   NA____

    Decision making and control are delegated to the lowest appropriate levels.

    Decision making and control are retained at inappropriately high levels.

30. Recognition

| 1 | 2 | 3 | 4 | 5 | 6 | 7 | 8 | 9 | 10 | NA____ |

We consistently acknowledge actions that support our strategies and goals.

We do not consistently acknowledge actions that support our strategies and goals.

31. Professional Development

| 1 | 2 | 3 | 4 | 5 | 6 | 7 | 8 | 9 | 10 | NA____ |

Professional development opportunities are limited, or individuals are frequently constrained from taking advantage of them.

XYZ is committed to professional development at all levels.

32. Creativity

| 1 | 2 | 3 | 4 | 5 | 6 | 7 | 8 | 9 | 10 | NA____ |

Individuals are encouraged to develop new ideas and to improve operational efficiency and effectiveness.

Individuals are discouraged from developing new ideas or from improving operational efficiency and effectiveness.

33. Risk Taking

| 1 | 2 | 3 | 4 | 5 | 6 | 7 | 8 | 9 | 10 | NA____ |

Managers discourage risk taking in support of the organizational mission and strategies.

Managers encourage risk taking in support of the organizational mission and strategies.

34. Cross-Departmental or Cross-Functional Work

| 1 | 2 | 3 | 4 | 5 | 6 | 7 | 8 | 9 | 10 | NA____ |

Individuals seem encouraged to work across departmental and functional lines to achieve their goals.

Individuals are not encouraged to work across departmental and functional lines.

35. Technology

     1   2   3   4   5   6   7   8   9   10   NA____

We effectively and proactively apply
technology to improve management
and operational effectiveness.

Our use of technology for management
or operational purposes is haphazard to
nonexistent.

36. Functions and Activities

     1   2   3   4   5   6   7   8   9   10   NA____

Some necessary functions and
activities are not properly planned or
are missing, duplicated, or not clearly
assigned.

All necessary functions and activities are
properly planned, clearly assigned, and
routinely fulfilled.

37. Roles and Responsibilities

     1   2   3   4   5   6   7   8   9   10   NA____

Roles and responsibilities are clear
and appropriate.

Roles and responsibilities are ambiguous
or inappropriate.

38. Administrative Support

     1   2   3   4   5   6   7   8   9   10   NA____

The administrative and secretarial
support is adequate.

The administrative and secretarial
support is not adequate.

39. Work Assignments

     1   2   3   4   5   6   7   8   9   10   NA____

I generally receive clear and
complete instructions when work
is assigned.

I generally do not receive clear and
complete instructions when work is
assigned.

40. Teamwork

     1   2   3   4   5   6   7   8   9   10   NA____

XYZ managers work effectively
together as a team.

XYZ managers do not work effectively
together as a team.

41. Work Priorities

| 1 | 2 | 3 | 4 | 5 | 6 | 7 | 8 | 9 | 10 | NA____ |

XYZ has set clear and understandable work priorities that are adhered to.

XYZ has no set clear and understandable work priorities that are adhered to.

42. Accountability

| 1 | 2 | 3 | 4 | 5 | 6 | 7 | 8 | 9 | 10 | NA____ |

Individuals are held accountable for use of resources and completing assigned tasks.

Individuals are not held accountable for use of resources and completing assigned tasks.

43. Program Knowledge

| 1 | 2 | 3 | 4 | 5 | 6 | 7 | 8 | 9 | 10 | NA____ |

Individuals are well informed about policies, regulations, and relevant standards.

Individuals have insufficient knowledge about policies, regulations, and relevant standards.

44. System Knowledge

| 1 | 2 | 3 | 4 | 5 | 6 | 7 | 8 | 9 | 10 | NA____ |

Individuals know how their assignment areas affect the work of others and fit into XYZ systems and processes.

Individuals do not know how their own work affects that of others and fits into XYZ systems and processes.

45. Organizational Knowledge

| 1 | 2 | 3 | 4 | 5 | 6 | 7 | 8 | 9 | 10 | NA____ |

The purpose and function of workgroups within XYZ is effectively communicated and understood.

The purpose and function of each workgroup within XYZ is not known and not understood.

46. Customer Service

| 1 | 2 | 3 | 4 | 5 | 6 | 7 | 8 | 9 | 10 | NA____ |

We know our customers and XYZ is a customer-service organization.

We do not know our customers and XYZ is not a customer-service organization.

Comments

Please comment on any significant strengths or weaknesses in the areas of leadership, management, organization, and culture. You may address issues not specifically raised in the questionnaire questions or expand on your responses to particular questionnaire items. As before, you may do this electronically or on paper, being sure to return the comments with your questionnaire.

V. Open Questions

A. What would you identify as XYZ's most important *strengths*?

1.

2.

3.

4.

5.

B. What would you identify as XYZ's most important *weaknesses*?

1.

2.

3.

4.

5.

C. If you could change anything about XYZ, what would it be?

1.

2.

3.

4.

5.

Thank you for your effort in completing this questionnaire.

Analyzing and Reporting Results of Internal and External Surveys

It is important to discuss your organization's internal and external survey results and explore their implications. What do the answers imply in terms of possible strategic or operational issues, concerns, or opportunities? What does the distribution of the answers imply? It is likely to show that your organization does very well with some stakeholders, clients, or customers but not others. Why is that?

Discussion of these results in facilitated sessions with a broad cross section of stakeholders can produce not only a good list of possible strategic and operational issues but typically many suggestions for strategies and action as well. Participation in discussing the results of these surveys usually heightens ownership of the issues, the strategic planning process, and the resulting strategic plan.

Do not be afraid to use customized versions of the surveys presented in Resources E and F and to discuss the results with stakeholders. The truth is that organizations and their stakeholders actually have few secrets. Most people are aware of the real underlying problems, and if they are not raised and discussed, the credibility of the strategic planning process is hurt and the real issues go unaddressed.

To assist people in making sense of the surveys, it is important to report the data in ways that are clear and easy to read. We suggest using graphs. Figure 6 illustrates how the XYZ Organization's results might be displayed for two questions, one from an external survey and one from an internal survey.

FIGURE 6

Reporting Survey Results with Graphics

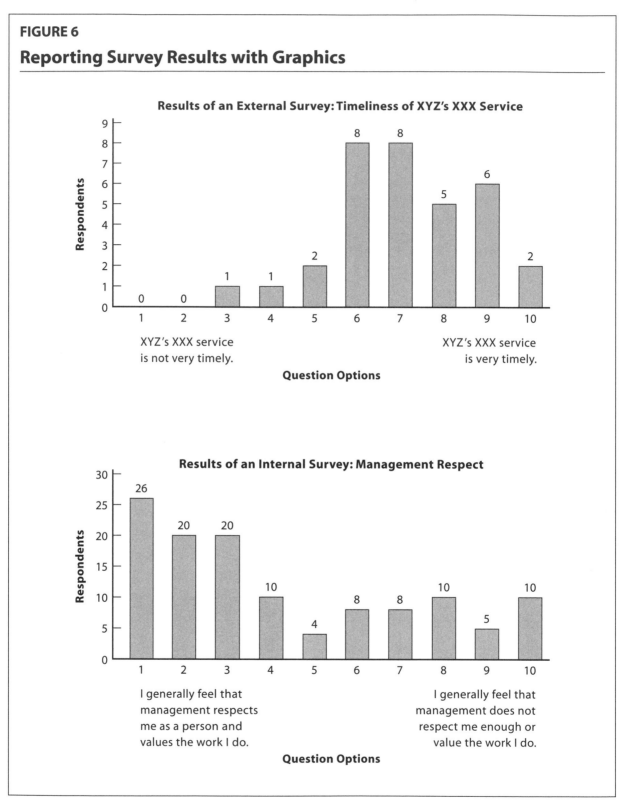

Results of an External Survey: Timeliness of XYZ's XXX Service

XYZ's XXX service is not very timely.

XYZ's XXX service is very timely.

Question Options

Results of an Internal Survey: Management Respect

I generally feel that management respects me as a person and values the work I do.

I generally feel that management does not respect me enough or value the work I do.

Question Options

Source: *This reporting format is presented as a model only. It has been modified from actual reports developed originally in 2001 by Farnum Alston and The Crescent Company, Bozeman, Montana. A report of this type must be tailored to fit the organization.*

Glossary

action plan   A plan for the day-to-day operation of an organization or an organizational unit over the next one to twelve months. It includes a prioritized list of proposed projects as well as plans for all projects that have been funded. Development of an action plan should never require more than two months. The action plan should be reviewed and updated weekly.

alignment   (1) The arrangement of things in a line, meaning in the organizational context that there should be a direct connection all the way from mission to operations on the ground and the production of desired outputs and outcomes. (2) The arrangement and adjustment of things so they are in a proper relationship to each other and therefore better coordination occurs. (3) Essential agreement among individuals, groups, and organizations involved in implementation about what should be done, how, and why.

champions   People having primary responsibility for managing strategic planning efforts on a day-to-day basis.

competencies   Capabilities, sets of actions, or strategies at which the organization is particularly good, or the resources (broadly conceived) on which it can draw to perform well in terms of its critical success factors. A competency is *the ability to do something well*. A *distinctive competency* is a competency that is very difficult for others to replicate and so it is a source of enduring organizational advantage. A *core competency* is central to the success of the organization; it is difficult for others to replicate and so is a source of enduring organizational advantage. A *distinctive core competency* is not only central to the success of the organization but helps the organization add more public value than alternative providers have. Examples of distinctive core competencies are ways of delivering services that are unique and especially valued by recipients, and ways of maintaining the organization's reputation and people's trust in it far in excess of what rivals can do. An *asset* is a resource that may be used to support a competency, distinctive competency, core competency, or distinctive core competency. A *distinctive asset* is a supportive resource that is unique to the organization. A *core distinctive asset* is a distinctive asset that is central to the achievement of the organization's business aspirations.

critical success factor   Something that the organization must do or a criterion it must meet in order to be successful in the eyes of its key stakeholders, especially those in its external environment.

decision making   The process of making an authoritative choice about what to do in a particular circumstance.

deliberation   Deliberation denotes careful, intentional, typically slow consideration of possible choices prior to choosing next steps. Both analysis and synthesis are typically involved, as is dialogue.

dialogue   Dialogue focuses on discovery and listening to each other. The purpose is to increase understanding by hearing what others think and why they think that way. This curiosity to discover each other's assumptions, judgments, values, attitudes, opinions, hopes, expectations, and fears helps everyone learn and creates new, shared understanding.

formative evaluation   An evaluation focused on program or project improvement, not on making summary judgments about effectiveness. Formative evaluation seeks to understand what is going on in a program or project, to analyze what is working and what is not, and to feed information and recommendations back to implementers about how to improve it.

goal   A long-term organizational target or direction of development. It states what the organization wants to accomplish or become over the next several years. Goals provide the basis for decisions about the nature, scope, and relative priorities of all projects and activities. Everything the organization does should help it move toward attainment of one or more goals.

implementation   The effort to realize in practice an organization's mission, goals, and strategies; the meeting of its mandates; continued organizational learning; and the ongoing creation of public value.

mandate   Something an organization is required to do (or not do), often imposed by an external actor. Mandates may be formal, such as laws, rules, or regulations, or informal, such as political mandates for change or deeply held public expectations. Mandates vary in what they require. Sometimes they require that a particular process or set of activities be followed; at other times they specify that a particular standard or outcome be achieved. Sometimes they simply authorize action in a specific area for very general purposes.

milestone   A significant date or event during execution of a project—often associated with the end of a phase or subphase.

mission statement   A statement of organizational purpose.

objective   A measurable target that must be met on the way to attaining a goal.

ongoing operations   Permanent endeavors that produce repetitive outputs, with resources assigned to the repeated accomplishment of basically the same sets of tasks, according to the standards institutionalized in a product or service life cycle.

outcomes   The end results, consequences, and ideally benefits of outputs for stakeholders, and the larger meanings attached to those outputs.

outputs   The actual things or final products produced by actions, behaviors, programs, projects, products, or services; the direct consequences produced by the implemented strategy, program, project, or other implementation element.

performance measure   A means of reasonably objectively assessing the results of programs, products, projects, or services.

public value   The public and nonprofit sector equivalent of *shareholder value*. Public value is what the organization does, can, or should create that the public (or parts of it) values in a collective sense. The focus is on shared or collective benefits.

sponsors   People (typically, top positional leaders) who have the prestige, power, and authority to commit the organization to strategic planning (and often implementation) and to hold people accountable for doing so.

stakeholder   Any person, group, or organization that can place a claim on an organization's attention, resources, or output, or is affected by that output.

strategic management   The integration of strategic planning and implementation across an organization (or other entity) in an ongoing way to enhance the fulfillment of mission, meeting of mandates, and sustained creation of public value.

strategic planning   A deliberative, disciplined effort to produce fundamental decisions and actions that shape and guide what an organization (or other entity) is, what it does, and why it does it. Strategic planning is an approach to dealing with the serious challenges that organizations, parts of organizations, collaborations, and communities face.

strategy   The means by which an organization intends to accomplish a goal or objective. It summarizes a pattern across policies, programs, projects, decisions, and resource allocations.

values   Principles, beliefs, and the like that form an important part of the foundation on which an organization operates. *Value statements* answer these questions: How do we want to conduct our business? How do we want to treat our key stakeholders? What do we really care about—that is, value? Values are a part of an organization's culture, so there may very well be a difference between the values people *espouse* and the values they actually follow *in practice*.

values statement   A description of the code of behavior (in relation to employees, other key stakeholders, and society at large) to which an organization adheres or aspires.

vision sketch   A brief description of what an organization will look like if it succeeds in implementing its strategies and achieving its full potential. A vision sketch is shorter and less detailed than a *vision of success*.

vision of success   A description of what an organization will look like if it succeeds in implementing its strategies and achieves its full potential. Often this statement includes the organization's mission, basic philosophy and core values, goals, basic strategies, performance criteria, important decision-making rules, and the ethical standards expected of all employees.

Bibliography

Allison, M., & Kaye, J. (1997). *Strategic planning for nonprofit organizations: A practical guide and workbook*. Hoboken, NJ: Wiley.

Barry, B. W. (1996). *Strategic planning workbook for nonprofit organizations*. Saint Paul, MN: Amherst H. Wilder Foundation.

Bryson, J. M. (1995). *Strategic planning for public and nonprofit organizations* (Rev. ed.) San Francisco: Jossey-Bass/Wiley.

Bryson, J. M. (2004). What to do when stakeholders matter: Stakeholder identification and analysis techniques. *Public Management Review, 6*(1), 21–53.

Bryson, J. M. (2011). *Strategic planning for public and nonprofit organizations* (4th ed.). San Francisco: Jossey-Bass/Wiley.

Bryson, J. M., Ackermann, F., & Eden, C. (2007). Putting the resource-based view of strategy and distinctive competencies to work in public organizations. *Public Administration Review, 67*(4), 702–717.

Bryson, J. M., Ackermann, F., Eden, C., & Finn, C. B. (2004). *Visible thinking: Unlocking causal mapping for practical business results*. Hoboken, NJ: Wiley.

Bryson, J. M., Anderson, S. R., & Alston F. K. (2011). *Implementing and sustaining your strategic plan*. San Francisco: Jossey-Bass/Wiley.

Bryson, J. M., & Crosby, B. C. (1992). *Leadership for the common good: Tackling public problems in a shared-power world*. San Francisco: Jossey-Bass/Wiley.

Bryson, J. M., Patton, M. Q., & Bowman, R. A. (2011). Working with evaluation stakeholders: A rationale, step-wise approach and toolkit. *Evaluation and Program Planning, 34*(1), 1–12.

Crosby, B. C., & Bryson, J. M. (2005). *Leadership for the common good: Tackling public problems in a shared-power world* (2nd ed.). San Francisco: Jossey-Bass/Wiley.

Eden, C., & Ackermann, F. (1998). *Making strategy: The journey of strategic management.* Thousand Oaks, CA: Sage.

Eden, C., & Ackermann, F. (2010). Competences, distinctive competences, and core competences. In R. Sanchez & A. Heene (Series Eds.), & R. Sanchez, A. Heene, & T. E. Zimmermann (Vol. Eds.), *Research in competence-based management: Vol. 5. A focused issue on identifying, building, and linking competences* (pp. 3–33). Bingley, UK: Emerald.

Eden, C., & Ackermann, F., with Brown, I. (2005). *The practice of making strategy.* Thousand Oaks, CA: Sage.

Holman, P., Devane, T., & Cady, S. (2007). *The change handbook: Group methods for shaping the future* (2nd ed.). San Francisco: Berrett-Koehler.

International Association for Public Participation. (2007). *Spectrum of public participation.* http:// www.iap2.org/associations/4748/files/IAP2%20Spectrum_vertical.pdf

Johnson, D. W., & Johnson, F. P. (2008). *Joining together: Group theory and group skills* (10th ed.). Upper Saddle River, NJ: Pearson Education.

Johnson, G., Scholes, K., & Whittington, R. (2008). *Exploring corporate strategy* (8th ed.). London: Financial Times/Prentice Hall.

Kouzes, J. M., & Posner, B. Z. (2002). *The leadership challenge* (3rd ed.). San Francisco: Jossey-Bass/Wiley.

Kouzes, J. M., & Posner, B. Z. (2008). *The leadership challenge* (4th ed.). San Francisco: Jossey-Bass/Wiley.

Mintzberg, H., Ahlstrand, B., & Lampel, J. (2009). *Strategy safari: A guided tour through the wilds of strategic management* (2nd ed.). London: Financial Times/Prentice Hall.

Mintzberg, H., & Westley, F. (1992). Cycles of organizational change. *Strategic Management Journal, 13,* 39–59.

Moynihan, D. P. (2008). *The dynamics of performance management.* Washington, DC: Georgetown University Press.

Nutt, P. C. (2002). *Why decisions fail.* San Francisco: Berrett-Koehler.

Nutt, P. C., & Backoff, R. W. (1992). *Strategic management of public and third sector organizations: A handbook for leaders.* San Francisco: Jossey-Bass/Wiley.

Schwarz, R. M. (2002). *The skilled facilitator: Practical wisdom for developing effective groups* (2nd ed.). San Francisco: Jossey-Bass/Wiley.

Shamir, B., Arthur, M., & House, R. (1994). The rhetoric of charismatic leadership: A theoretical extension, a case study, and implications for research. *The Leadership Quarterly, 5*(1), 25–42.

Spencer, L. (1996). *Winning through participation.* Dubuque, IA: Kendall/Hunt.